W9-AAE-634

INTRODUCING
ISSUES
WITH

OPPOSING  VIEWPOINTS®

TERRORISM

INTRODUCING ISSUES WITH

OPPOSING VIEWPOINTS®

TERRORISM

Other books in the Introducing Issues
with Opposing Viewpoints series:

TERRORISM

Lauri S. Friedman, *Book Editor*

Bruce Glassman, *Vice President*
Bonnie Szumski, *Publisher*
Helen Cothran, *Managing Editor*

OPPOSING
VIEWPOINTS®
SERIES

GREENHAVEN PRESS
An imprint of Thomson Gale, a part of The Thomson Corporation

Detroit • New York • San Francisco • San Diego • New Haven, Conn. • Waterville, Maine • London • Munich

© 2005 Thomson Gale, a part of The Thomson Corporation.

Thomson and Star Logo are trademarks and Gale and Greenhaven Press are registered trademarks used herein under license.

For more information, contact
Greenhaven Press
27500 Drake Rd.
Farmington Hills, MI 48331-3535
Or you can visit our Internet site at http://www.gale.com

Picture Credits: Cover: © Reuters/CORBIS; Johnny Bivera/U.S. Navy, 86; Alta I. Cutler/U.S. Navy, 20 (inset); © Larry Downing/Reuters/Landov, 19; EPA/Landov, 90; Geoff Green/Landov, 16; Samantha Jones/U.S. Marine Corps, 95; Faleh Kheiber/Reuters/Landov, 27; Kevin Lamarque/Reuters/Landov, 67; Faisal Mahmood/Reuters/Landov, 49; Eli J. Medellin/U.S. Navy, 72 (inset); © Francoise de Mulder/CORBIS, 61; William Philpott/Reuters/Landov, 74; PR Newswire NEWSWEEK, 25; © Reuters/CORBIS, 38, 45, 56, 103; © Reuters/Landov, 28, 37 (both), 43, 94; Reuters/U.S. Navy-Lyle G. Becker /Landov, 57; Mohammed Saber/EPA/Landov, 40, 46; Mohammed Salem/Reuters/Landov, 52; © Sana/Reuters/CORBIS, 88; Sue Santillan, 33, 36, 62, 68, 70, 76; © Mike Simons/CORBIS, 80; © S. Staveris/Apeiron/CORBIS SYGMA, 64; Larry R. Smith/U.S. Navy, 20 (main); Helene C. Stikkel/U.S. Department of Defense, 101; UPI/Landov, 51; U.S. Coast Guard, 14–15, 72 (main); U.S. Dept. of Homeland Security, 13; Jim Watson/U.S. Navy, 12

LIBRARY OF CONGRESS CATALOGING-IN-PUBLICATION DATA

Terrorism/Lauri S. Friedman, book editor.
   p. cm. — (Introducing issues with opposing viewpoints)
  Includes bibliographical references and index.
ISBN 0-7377-3225-3 (lib. bdg. : alk. paper)
  1. Terrorism. 2. War on terrorism, 2001– . 3. Terrorism—United States—Prevention.
I. Friedman, Lauri S. II. Series.
  HV6431.T45698 2005
  973.931—dc22

                                                     2005040416

Printed in the United States of America

CONTENTS

I ndulging in a wide spectrum of ideas, beliefs, and perspectives is a critical cornerstone of democracy. After all, it is often debates over differences of opinion, such as whether to legalize abortion, how to treat prisoners, or when to enact the death penalty that shape our society and drive it forward. Such diversity of thought is frequently regarded as the hallmark of a healthy and civilized culture, whereas ideological insulation is perceived as dangerous and negligent. As the Reverend Clifford Schutjer of the First Congregational Church in Mansfield, Ohio, declared in a 2001 sermon, "Surrounding oneself with only like-minded people, restricting what we listen to or read only to what we find agreeable is irresponsible. Refusing to entertain doubts once we make up our minds is a subtle but deadly form of arrogance." With this advice in mind, Introducing Issues with Opposing Viewpoints books aim to open readers' minds to the critically divergent views that comprise our world's most important debates.

Introducing Issues with Opposing Viewpoints simplifies for students the enormous and often overwhelming mass of material now available to us via print and electronic media. Collected in every volume is an array of opinions that capture the essence of a particular controversy or topic. Introducing Issues with Opposing Viewpoints books embody the spirit of nineteenth-century journalist Charles A. Dana's axiom: "Fight for your opinions, but do not believe that they contain the whole truth, or the only truth." Absorbing such contrasting opinions teaches students to analyze the strength of an argument and compare it to its opposition. From this process readers can inform and strengthen their own opinions, or be exposed to new information that will change their minds. Some views presented are familiar and widely held; others are more unusual, but no less valid. Other opinions may be utterly controversial, yet included to expose students to the full gamut of ideas that are unearthed when one engages in debate. Introducing Issues with Opposing Viewpoints is a mosaic of these different voices. The authors are statesmen, pundits, academics, journalists, corporations, and ordinary people who have felt compelled to share their experiences and ideas in a public forum. Their words have been collected from newspapers, journals, books, speeches, interviews, and the Internet, the fastest growing body of opinionated material in the world.

Introducing Issues with Opposing Viewpoints shares many of the well-known features of its critically acclaimed parent series, Opposing Viewpoints. The articles are presented in a pro/con format, allowing readers to absorb divergent perspectives side by side. Active reading questions preface each viewpoint, requiring the student to approach the material thoughtfully and carefully. Useful charts, graphs, and cartoons supplement each article and offer readers multiple formats for gleaning information on the topic. A thorough introduction provides readers with crucial background on an issue. An annotated bibliography points the reader toward articles, books, and Web sites that contain additional information on the topic. An appendix of organizations to contact contains a wide variety of charities, nonprofit organizations, political groups, and private enterprises that each hold a position on the issue at hand. Finally, a comprehensive index allows readers to locate content quickly and efficiently.

Introducing Issues with Opposing Viewpoints is also significantly different from Opposing Viewpoints. As the series title implies, its presentation will help introduce students to the concept of opposing viewpoints, and learn to use this material to aid in critical writing and debate. The series' four-color, accessible format makes the books attractive and inviting to readers of all levels. In addition, each viewpoint has been carefully edited to maximize a reader's understanding of the content. Short but thorough viewpoints capture the essence of an argument. A substantial, thought-provoking essay question placed at the end of each viewpoint asks the student to further investigate the issues raised in the viewpoint, compare and contrast two authors' arguments, or consider how one might go about forming an opinion on the topic at hand. Each viewpoint contains sidebars that include at-a-glance information and handy statistics. A Facts About section located in the back of the book further supplies students with relevant facts and figures.

Following in the tradition of the Opposing Viewpoints series, Greenhaven Press continues to provide readers with invaluable exposure to the controversial issues that shape our world. As John Stuart Mill once wrote: "The only way in which a human being can make some approach to knowing the whole of a subject is by hearing what can be said about it by persons of every variety of opinion and studying all modes in which it can be looked at by every character of mind. No wise man ever acquired his wisdom in any mode but this." It is to this principle that Introducing Issues with Opposing Viewpoints books are dedicated.

INTRODUCTION

"Although we can and should take comfort in the fact that America has not been attacked again, that does not necessarily mean that all of the actions we have taken have prevented an attack. It could simply be that al Qaeda has not chosen to attack. Unfortunately, we are at a loss to know the explanation."

—Charles V. Peña, director of defense policy studies at the Cato Institute

The events of September 11, 2001, were shockingly abrupt, horrifyingly dramatic: Only once before had America been attacked on its own soil, at Pearl Harbor. Many Americans were left shaken, some nearly paralyzed by fear of another attack. In the years since the attacks, the U.S. government has made the fight against terror its single greatest priority and has undertaken two wars in its name. The media have devoted huge amounts of money and time to covering terrorism-related stories, while Americans incessantly discuss the war on terror, its progress, flaws, and successes. The attack on America will never be forgotten, but, many people ask, what is the likelihood that it could or would happen again?

Whether America needs to be concerned about a future attack is hotly debated. On any given day, Americans read a variety of news sources and get very different impressions regarding the seriousness of the problem. By some accounts, terrorists are thriving in our midst and abroad, constantly plotting their next attack. By other accounts, terrorism is no more or less prevalent than other crimes that must be tackled. Some people claim that the fact America has not been victim to a second attack proves the government has adequately protected the public. They contend that the unprecedented attention paid to security after September 11 has warded off future attacks. Others, however, argue that the absence of attacks is more likely because terrorists have not attempted any and warn that America is still dangerously vulnerable to terrorism. Still others regard terrorism as a problem that has been exaggerated by a hypervigilant public.

To better inform the public about the threat of a future terrorist attack, the Department of Homeland Security (DHS) established the Homeland Security Advisory System in 2002. This is a five-tiered chart that ranks the level of the current terrorist threat. Alerts can be green (the lowest risk), blue, yellow, orange, or red (which means the risk of a terrorist attack is severe). When the system was unveiled on March 12, 2002, former DHS secretary Tom Ridge said, "The Homeland Security Advisory System . . . provides clear, easy to understand factors which help measure threat. And most importantly, it empowers government and citizens to take actions to address the threat."

But despite these origins, it soon became clear that the color-coded alert system further confused Americans' perceptions of the terrorist threat.

A New York City firefighter looks on as a bulldozer clears debris around a small section of the World Trade Center left standing after the terrorist attacks of September 11, 2001.

Immediately after they began to be issued, threat alerts became controversial. For one, they tended to be vague, containing little in the way of hard details and specific information. When these kinds of ambiguous alerts were issued, people tended to either frantically panic or cynically disregard them. The alerts were also controversial because of their frequency; in the year and a half after the system was created, the threat level switched between yellow and orange half a dozen times, causing people to disagree over whether the alerts were truly warranted. Many Americans fur-

Many Americans criticized the five-tiered Homeland Security Advisory System as too vague.

ther complained that the message of the warnings was contradictory—people were put on alert for a possible terrorist attack, but then advised to go about their lives as they normally would. Still others were suspicious that alerts were issued to either divert attention away from or coincide with certain political events.

On August 5, 2004, the problems surrounding the threat advisory system were made clear when the threat level was again raised to orange, the second highest level. The nation was put on high alert in response to intelligence that indicated terrorists may have been interested in attacking financial buildings in New York, New Jersey, and Washington, D.C. When the intelligence that precipitated the alert was further scrutinized, it became unclear whether it was newly acquired information that indicated an imminent attack or old, unspecific information that was available even prior to the September 11 attacks. Americans, particularly those living and working in the targeted areas, found themselves scared, frustrated, or lacking confidence

A Coast Guard officer on the deck of a security boat stands watch over lower Manhattan during the 2004 Republican National Convention.

that the alerts contained useful information. In response to the orange alert, the *New York Times* opined,

> [President] Bush should junk the color bars, which are now of use mostly to late-night comedians. Ordinary people have no way of calibrating their lives to the color ladder. It does them no good to be told to be scared, more scared or really scared, especially when they are also being told to act as if nothing's wrong. Unless the

government is prepared to tell people to stay home from work, there's no reason to keep lighting the terror lamps. What we need is information that we can use, not another shot of adrenaline.

Others, however, considered the release of any information helpful for keeping Americans vigilant against attack. An editorial in the *Buffalo News,* for example, had this to say about the August orange alert:

Nearly three years after 9/11 . . . the alert was a stomach-churning reminder that this target-rich country has enemies devoted to inflicting as much pain as they can, in as many ways as they can. That reminder cannot be strong enough, or made often enough. It would be unfortunate if the public discounts the danger. . . . [It is] better to be warned than not.

Clearly, Americans have yet to agree on what actions will best ensure the safety of the nation, and even whether we can ever be truly safe. In the coming years, Americans will need to find a way to be vigilant against terrorism while at the same time avoiding widespread panic and overreaction. The articles presented in *Introducing Issues with Opposing Viewpoints: Terrorism* offer insight into the threat terrorism poses and the various debates that surround the issue today.

CHAPTER 1

Is Terrorism a Serious Threat?

On September 11, 2001, smoke billows from the north tower of the World Trade Center as a second hijacked plane strikes the south tower.

The War on Terror Has Made America Safer from Terrorism

George W. Bush

"We are waging a broad and unrelenting war against terror."

Before George W. Bush became the forty-third president of the United States, he was the governor of Texas from 1996 to 2000. The following viewpoint is taken from a speech delivered by President Bush to employees of the Y-12 National Security Complex in Oak Ridge, Tennessee. In the viewpoint the president argues that terrorists pose a grave danger and are determined to attack America in whatever way they can. To combat this threat, Bush claims the United States has effectively acted to reduce the terrorist threat around the world. President Bush also argues that making alliances with nations such as Pakistan and Saudi Arabia has reduced the terrorists' capabilities in those countries. Although terrorists still wish harm upon America, President Bush argues that their numbers have been reduced, and for this the United States is safer.

George W. Bush, remarks at the Oak Ridge National Laboratory, Oak Ridge, Tennessee, July 12, 2004.

A merica's determination to actively oppose the threats of our time was formed and fixed on September the 11th, 2001. On that day we saw the cruelty of the terrorists, and we glimpsed the future they intend for us. They intend to strike the United States to the limits of their power. They seek weapons of mass destruction to kill Americans on an even greater scale. And this danger is increased when outlaw regimes build or acquire weapons of mass destruction and maintain ties to terrorist groups.

This is our danger, but not our fate. America has the resources and the strength and the resolve to overcome this threat. We are waging a broad and unrelenting war against terror, and an active campaign against proliferation. We refuse to live in fear. We are making steady progress.

To protect our people, we're staying on the offensive against threats within our own country. We are using the Patriot Act [which expands the powers of law enforcement agencies] to track terrorist activity and to break up terror cells. Intelligence and law enforcement officials are sharing information as never before. We've transformed the mission of the FBI [Federal Bureau of Investigation] to focus on preventing terrorism. Every element of our homeland security plan is critical, because the terrorists are ruthless and resourceful—and we know they're preparing to attack us again. It's not possible to guarantee perfect security in our vast, free nation. But I can assure our fellow Americans, many fine professionals in intelligence and national security and homeland security and law enforcement are working around the clock doing everything they can to protect the country. And we're grateful to them all. . . .

Removing Threats Abroad

Three years ago [in 2001], the nation of Afghanistan was the home base of [the terrorist group] al Qaeda, a country ruled by the Taliban,

In July 2004 President Bush speaks at the Y-12 National Security Complex in Oak Ridge, Tennessee, of America's need to defend itself from the grave threat of terrorism.

one of the most backward and brutal regimes of modern history. Schooling was denied girls. Women were whipped in the streets and executed in a sports stadium. Millions lived in fear. With protection from the Taliban, al Qaeda and its associates trained, indoctrinated, and sent forth thousands of killers to set up terror cells in dozens of countries, including our own.

Today, Afghanistan is a world away from the nightmare of the Taliban. That country has a good and just President. Boys and girls are being educated. Many refugees have returned home to rebuild their country, and a presidential election is scheduled for this fall [2004]. The terror camps are closed and the Afghan government is helping us to hunt the Taliban and terrorists in remote regions. Today, because we acted to liberate Afghanistan, a threat has been removed, and the American people are safer.

Three years ago, Pakistan was one of the few countries in the world that recognized the Taliban regime. Al Qaeda was active and recruiting in Pakistan, and was not seriously opposed. Pakistan served as a transit point for al Qaeda terrorists leaving Afghanistan on missions

A technician inspects missiles (inset) before loading them onto an F/A-18C fighter jet heading for a mission over Afghanistan.

of murder. Yet the United States was not on good terms with Pakistan's military and civilian leaders—the very people we would need to help shut down al Qaeda operations in that part of the world.

Today, the governments of the United States and Pakistan are working closely in the fight against terror. President [Pervez] Musharraf is a friend of our country, who helped us capture Khalid Sheik Mohammed, the operational planner behind the September the 11th attacks. And Pakistani forces are rounding up terrorists along their nation's western border. Today, because we're working with the Pakistani leaders, Pakistan is an ally in the war on terror, and the American people are safer.

Three years ago, terrorists were well-established in Saudi Arabia. Inside that country, fund-raisers and other facilitators gave al Qaeda financial and logistical help, with little scrutiny or opposition. Today, after the attacks in Riyadh [the Saudi capital] and elsewhere, the Saudi government knows that al Qaeda is its enemy. Saudi Arabia is working hard to shut down the facilitators and financial supporters of terrorism. The government has captured or killed many first-tier leaders of the al Qaeda organization in Saudi Arabia. . . . Today, because Saudi Arabia has seen the danger and has joined the war on terror, the American people are safer.

Before the Bar of Justice

Three years ago, the ruler of Iraq [Saddam Hussein] was a sworn enemy of America, who provided safe haven for terrorists, used weapons of mass destruction, and turned his nation into a prison. Saddam Hussein was not just a dictator; he was a proven mass murderer who refused to account for weapons of mass murder. Every responsible nation recognized this threat, and knew it could not go on forever. . . .

Today, the dictator who caused decades of death and turmoil, who twice invaded his neighbors, who harbored terrorist leaders, who used chemical weapons on innocent men, women, and children, is finally before the bar of justice. Iraq, which once had the worst government in the Middle East, is now becoming an example of reform to the region. And Iraqi security forces are fighting beside coalition troops to defeat the terrorists and foreign fighters who threaten their nation and the world. Today, because America and our coalition helped to end the violent regime of Saddam Hussein, and because we're helping to raise a peaceful democracy in its place, the American people are safer. . . .

> **FAST FACT**
>
> Under the Taliban regime, Afghan women could not leave their home without a male escort. When they did, they had to be covered from head to toe in a garment called a *burqa,* which concealed all of their skin except for their hands.

America Is Safer

Three years ago, the world was very different. Terrorists planned attacks, with little fear of discovery or reckoning. Outlaw regimes supported terrorists and defied the civilized world, without shame and with few consequences. Weapons proliferators sent their deadly shipments and grew wealthy, encountering few obstacles to their trade.

The world changed on September the 11th, and since that day, we have changed the world. We are leading a steady, confident, systematic campaign against the dangers of our time. There are still terrorists who plot against us, but the ranks of their leaders are thinning, and they know what fate awaits them. There are still regimes actively supporting the terrorists, but fewer than there used to be. There are still outlaw regimes pursuing weapons of mass destruction, but the world no longer looks the other way. Today, because America has acted, and because America has led, the forces of terror and tyranny have suffered defeat after defeat, and America and the world are safer.

EVALUATING THE AUTHORS' VIEWS ON ERADICATING TERRORISTS:

In the viewpoint you just read, the author uses the fact that multiple terrorists have been captured or killed to argue that terrorism is decreasing. The author of the next viewpoint, however, compares terrorists to a mythical beast known as the hydra. The hydra was a monster that the Greeks believed had many heads; for every head that was chopped off, two would grow back in its place. The following viewpoint likens terrorists to the hydra, arguing that whenever a terrorist is captured or killed, new ones are inspired to take their place. After reading both viewpoints, do you believe that it is possible to eradicate all terrorists? Why or why not?

The War on Terror Has Not Made America Safer from Terrorism

Ted Rall

> "The invasions of Afghanistan and Iraq have . . . vastly increased the likelihood of future Sept. 11s."

In the following viewpoint, Ted Rall argues that the war on terrorism has endangered America. He explores the wars that were undertaken in Afghanistan and Iraq, and cites numerous financial, social, and military problems that beset both places. He insists that America's failure to provide security and basic services to the citizens of these countries has produced an anger and frustration that has inspired an increase in anti-Americanism. The author views other tactics designed to make America safe, such as fingerprinting Muslim tourists or creating large bureaucracies, as failed efforts that have only resulted in squandered money or international embarrassment. Thus far, the author concludes, America's war on terror has not resulted in any additional security; to do so it must abandon these failed tactics and embark on a new path.

Ted Rall is the author of *Gas War: The Truth Behind the American Occupation of Afghanistan.* He is a regular contributor to the *Progressive Populist,* from which the following viewpoint is taken.

Ted Rall, "Bush's Smoke and Mirrors Endangers USA," *Progressive Populist,* vol. 9, June 15, 2003. Copyright © 2003 by Universal Press Syndicate. Reproduced by permission.

AS YOU READ, CONSIDER THE FOLLOWING QUESTIONS:
1. What evidence does the author cite to argue that the wars in Iraq and Afghanistan have failed?
2. What are three ways the author suggests the war on terror could be improved?
3. Why is Rall convinced that going after individual terrorists is a waste of time?

We've killed thousands of Muslims and taken over two of their countries. We're spending billions of dollars to make it easier for our government to spy on us. But we haven't caught Osama [bin Laden], al Qaeda is doing better than ever and airport security is still a sick joke. So when are Americans going to demand a real war on terrorism?

An Expensive and Pointless Game of Whack-a-Mole

Recent suicide bombings in Riyadh [Saudi Arabia] and Casablanca [Morocco] proved with bloody eloquence that al Qaeda and similar extremist groups are anything but "on the run," as [President] George W. Bush puts it. Bush's tactics are a 100% failure, yet his band of clueless Christian soldiers continues to go after mosquitoes with shotguns. "So far," Bush furiously spun after the latest round of attacks, "nearly one-half of al Qaeda's senior operatives have been captured or killed," promising to "remain on the hunt until they are all brought to justice."

Can Bush really be this stupid? All underground organizations, including al Qaeda, employ a loose hierarchical structure. No individual member is indispensable, so the capture of even a high-ranking official cannot compromise the group. Each lost member is instantly replaced by the next man down in his cell. It doesn't matter whether we catch half, three-quarters or all of al Qaeda's leadership—hunting down individual terrorists is an expensive and pointless game of whack-a-mole. Only Allah [God] knows how

> **FAST FACT**
>
> In August 2004, U.S. forces stationed in Iraq were attacked an average of 70 times a day.

many eager recruits have sprung up, hydra-like, to fill [terrorist master-mind] Khalid Sheikh Mohammad's flip-flops.

The Afghanistan and Iraq Wars Have Been Disastrous

Senator and [former] Democratic presidential candidate Bob Graham caught heat for calling the war on Iraq "a distraction" from the war on terrorism, but he was far too kind. The invasions of Afghanistan [in 2001] and Iraq [in 2003] have replaced a real war on terrorism, and they've vastly increased the likelihood of future Sept. 11s. Bombing

Although Osama bin Laden became the most wanted man in the world after the September 11 attacks, the al Qaeda leader has eluded capture.

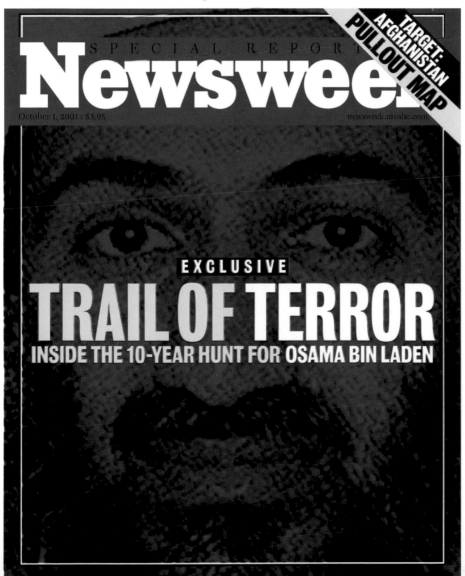

Afghanistan scattered bin Laden, his lieutenants and their foot soldiers everywhere from Chechnya to Sudan to China's Xinjiang province [all places of terrorist activity]. . . . With radical Shi'ite [a sect of Islam] clerics like the Ayatollah Mohammad Baqer al-Hakim poised to fill the post-Saddam [Hussein] power vacuum, Iraq could become . . . an anarchic collection of fiefdoms run by extremist warlords happy to host training camps for terrorist organizations.

"We're much safer," [former director of Homeland Security] Tom Ridge claims. If this is safety, give me danger.

Taking over Iraq and Afghanistan didn't score us any new fans among Muslims. We could have won them over with carefully crafted occupations, but chose instead to allow the two states to disintegrate into chaos and civil war.

Chaos and Incompetence

Rarely have incompetence and cheapness been wed with such impressively disastrous results. In Afghanistan, we paid off warlords whom we should have dropped bombs upon. Puppet president Hamid Karzai is threatening to abdicate his Kabul city-state because "there is no money in the government treasury." One of Karzai's ministers warns the *New York Times:* "Very soon we will see armed conflict."

As *USA Today* reported on May 7 [2004], "Iraqis say they view the US military with suspicion, anger and frustration. Many even say life was in some ways better under the regime of Saddam Hussein; the streets, they say, were safer, jobs more secure, food more plentiful and electricity and water supplies reliable." That's not the message we want on [the Arab news network] Al Jazeera TV—whose Baghdad correspondent, in the ultimate case of PR [public relations] gone bad, we assassinated in Iraq.

"Governance is a long-term process," says Bush administration reconstruction official Chris Milligan, but that's just another lame excuse. The truth is that we haven't even tried to restore law and order, much less govern. The Pentagon plans to leave just two divisions—30,000 men—to patrol Iraq. That's significantly fewer than the 50,000 peacekeeping troops NATO [North Atlantic Treaty Organization] stationed in Kosovo [during a war in 1999]—a nation less than one-fifth the size of Iraq. Some 95% of Afghanistan has no peacekeepers whatsoever, with fewer than 8,000 in Kabul.

We're sleeping soundly . . . but the guys who hate us so much they're willing to die to make their point are industriously exploiting our stu-

Anti-American demonstrators take to the streets of Baghdad. Many Muslims oppose American involvement in Iraq and Afghanistan.

pidity to sign up new jihadis [holy warriors]. "Since the United States invaded Iraq in March," the *Times* quoted top administration honchos on May 16 [2004], "the [al Qaeda] network has experienced a spike in recruitment. 'There is an increase in radical fundamentalism all over the world,' said a senior counterterrorism official based in Europe.". . .

The War on Terror Has Not Worked

It's still early in this game. Shut down the bloated and pointless Homeland Security bureaucracy—since it doesn't include the CIA and FBI it didn't stop interagency squabbling—and apply the money

Detainees bound in handcuffs are kept on their knees in a holding area of Camp X-Ray in Guantánamo Bay, Cuba.

we'll save into a fully-funded rebuilding of Iraq and Afghanistan. Stop squandering money and our civil rights on boneheaded data-mining schemes like Total Information Awareness (now renamed Terrorism Information Awareness) [which collects information about people in America], and recruit some old-fashioned spies to infiltrate extremist groups. Charge the detainees [from the war on terror being held indefinitely at Guantánamo Bay, Cuba] with a crime or send them home; their legal limbo is an international embarrassment. Stop fingerprinting Muslim tourists—it's insulting and does nothing to prevent terrorists from entering the country. Quit supporting brutal anti-American military dictators like Pakistan's Pervez Musharraf, whose oppressed subjects rightly blame us for their misery.

"The only way to deal with [terrorists] is to bring them to justice," Bush says. "You can't talk to them, you can't negotiate with them, you must find them." He couldn't be more mistaken. We'll never find them all. And while we shouldn't negotiate with those who call us the Great Satan [a name Islamic militants use to refer to the United States] we must talk to the millions of Muslims who watch the news every night. Their donations keep al Qaeda going. If we want them to stop financing the terrorists, we'd better stop acting like a Great Satan.

EVALUATING THE AUTHORS' ARGUMENTS:

Authors George W. Bush and Ted Rall both believe that terrorists pose a dangerous threat to America. But they disagree that actions taken since September 11, 2001, have effectively made America safer. After reading both viewpoints, do you believe that the war on terror has made America more or less safe? Why?

We Have Overestimated the Terrorist Threat

Bart Kosko

"We have overestimated— grossly overestimated— the terrorist threat."

In the following viewpoint, Bart Kosko suggests that the threat of terrorism has been exaggerated. He notes an absence of terrorist attacks in the three years following the attacks of September 11, 2001, and points out that no terrorist attacks have been attempted at high-profile events such as the 2004 summer Olympics. He notes that the rate of terrorism is so low, in fact, that people are more likely to be murdered or be the victim of a car accident. According to the author, these facts do not prove the United States is winning the war on terror. Instead, he argues that there are probably very few terrorists who pose a threat to the United States. The lack of terrorist attacks is due to the fact that the danger of such an attack is low.

Bart Kosko is a professor of electrical engineering at the University of Southern California, where he teaches probability and statistics. He is the author of eight books, including *Heaven in a Chip,* and numerous articles that are frequently published in the *Los Angeles Times,* from which this viewpoint was taken.

AS YOU READ, CONSIDER THE FOLLOWING QUESTIONS:
1. What explanation does the author offer for the fact that there were no terrorist attacks in the three years following September 11, 2001?
2. According to Kosko, what is at stake when governments "play it safe" on the issue of terrorism?
3. What do you think the author means when he describes shark bites and terrorist bombings as "vivid threats"?

J ust what is the evidence for this alleged terrorist threat that now dominates foreign affairs and the presidential election? The third anniversary of the 9-11 attacks on the Pentagon and World Trade Center has come and gone without any terrorist attacks in the United States for three years. No terrorists attacked the [2004] summer Olympics in Greece as so many feared. Nor did they attack the [2004] Republican Convention in New York. And the big statistical picture of terrorism has changed little in years.

Deaths due to terrorism worldwide have increased somewhat lately (especially after the school attack in Russia [in which Chechen terrorists killed 360 people in September 2004]). But according to the [U.S.] State Department's annual report "Patterns of Global Terrorism" the number still remains on the order of only about a thousand deaths per year—a small fraction of the 15,000 or so murders each year in the U.S.

> **FAST FACT**
>
> According to statisticians, Americans have a greater chance of getting struck by lightning or being killed in a car accident than dying in a terrorist attack.

Overestimating the Terrorist Threat

The Bush Administration and many others interpret these facts to support their conclusion that the government is winning the "war on terror"—even as 9-11 culprit Osama bin Laden still roams free and threatens from afar.

There may well have been some attacks by now if not for the government's stepped-up security at home and its vigorous anti-terrorism efforts abroad. We don't know. We do know that studies of our statistical competency show both that we systematically overestimate the probability of vivid threats such as shark bites and terrorist bombings and that we poorly estimate the probability of rare events such as terrorists getting nuclear bombs or other catastrophic weapons.

The comparative absence of terrorism also supports the very different conclusion that we have overestimated—grossly overestimated—the terrorist threat. We may be winning a war against terrorism simply because there are few terrorists who are credible threats to the U.S. So we may have traded substantial civil liberties and international goodwill for more security than we need—and the next attack may lead us to overreact even further.

Negative Evidence

This conclusion involves a subtle type of formal reasoning called *negative* evidence: sometimes a search that finds nothing is evidence that there is nothing.

Suppose you shop in a store and then can't find your car keys. How much of the store must you search before you conclude the keys are not there? The negative evidence for this conclusion grows as the search widens and finds nothing.

Source: LaBan. © 2001 by Terry LaBan. Reproduced by permission.

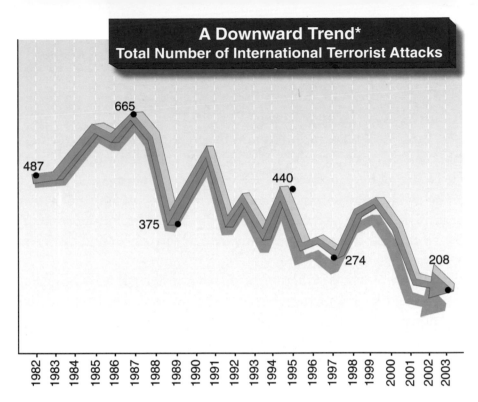

A Downward Trend*
Total Number of International Terrorist Attacks

665

487

440

375

274

208

1982 1983 1984 1985 1986 1987 1988 1989 1990 1991 1992 1993 1994 1995 1996 1997 1998 1999 2000 2001 2002 2003

Source: U.S. Department of State. *Numbers released by the Office of the Coordinator for Counterterrorism, June 22, 2004.

The strength of the negative evidence depends on the size and complexity of the search area. We have good negative evidence that there is no Loch Ness monster because no sonar sweep of the Scottish lake has found such a creature. We have less good negative evidence that there is no Bigfoot because we have not fully searched the larger and more complex area of pine forests in Northern California. And we have no good negative evidence at all that we are alone in the cosmos because we have just started to search the vast heavens for signs of structured energy.

The Iraq War gives a telling example of negative evidence. The coalition forces still cannot find the alleged stockpiles of weapons of mass destruction many believed Iraq had before the U.S. invasion. The weapons may be there but the negative evidence that they are not grows stronger each day as a wider search finds nothing. This negative evidence is almost conclusive.

This raises an important point of logic about the Iraq War: Almost everyone overestimated Saddam's military power despite the greatest level of digital surveillance in history. Logic demands that some of our assumptions are wrong. And a good candidate is our collective estimate of the strength of global terrorism.

Incentives to Exaggerate

The Bush Administration has said in effect that it was better to be safe than sorry with terrorist threats in Iraq and at home. The trouble is that all bureaucracies have a well-known incentive to over rely on being safe than sorry. No one wants to risk approving a new drug or airplane design that has even a slight chance of killing someone even if the new drug can save many lives or the new design can greatly increase flight efficiency.

A related problem is that terrorists have an incentive to exaggerate their strength in order to terrorize their opponents and to attract recruits and donations—remember the Symbionese Liberation "Army" and its 7-headed-cobra logo?[1] The result is an inadvertent global . . . equilibrium where governments play it safe by overestimating the terrorist threat while terrorists oblige by overestimating their power. A tight presidential race only heightens these perverse incentives all round.

Restricting civil liberties just makes it worse. It may help fight terrorists but it also encourages them to attack because it results in more terrorist bang for the buck.

The bottom line is this: There will always be terrorists and legitimate efforts to catch and kill them. But meanwhile the bigger statistical threat comes from the driver next to you who is talking on a cell phone.

EVALUATING THE AUTHOR'S REASONING:

The author employs a type of reasoning he calls "negative evidence" to suggest that the threat of terrorism is overstated. What is the idea behind negative evidence? Do you think this line of reasoning is useful when assessing the threat of terrorism? Why or why not?

1. A small handful of media-savvy radicals in the 1970s convinced much of the media and the nation that they were an "army."

Weapons of Mass Destruction Pose a Serious Threat

Nicholas D. Kristof

"Unless we act more aggressively, we will get a wake-up call from a nuclear explosion."

In the following viewpoint, Nicholas D. Kristof argues that terrorists are trying to obtain weapons of mass destruction to launch a deadly attack against the United States. He warns that terrorists could get their hands on unguarded nuclear weapons in Russia or buy them from rogue nations such as Pakistan or Iran. To prevent the destruction that would result from such an attack, the author urges the U.S. government to secure weapons sites in Russia and negotiate with rogue nations in order to curb the spread of nuclear weapons.

Nicholas D. Kristof is a columnist for the *New York Times.* He is the coauthor of *China Wakes: The Struggle for the Soul of a Rising Power* and *Thunder from the East: Portrait of a Rising Asia.*

AS YOU READ, CONSIDER THE FOLLOWING QUESTIONS:
1. According to the author, how many nations are known to possess nuclear weapons?
2. Who is Abdul Qadeer Khan?
3. According to the author, what effect would a ten-kiloton nuclear bomb have if exploded in New York City?

A 10-kiloton nuclear bomb (a pipsqueak in weapons terms) is smuggled into Manhattan [New York City] and explodes at Grand Central [train station]. Some 500,000 people are killed, and the U.S. suffers $1 trillion in direct economic damage.

That scenario, cited in a report last year [2003] from the John F. Kennedy School of Government at Harvard, could be a glimpse of our future. We urgently need to control nuclear materials to forestall that threat, but in this war on proliferation, we're now slipping backward. President [George W.] Bush (after ignoring the issue before [September 11, 2001]) now forcefully says the right things—but still doesn't do enough.

"We're losing the war on proliferation," Andrew F. Krepinevich Jr., a military expert and executive director of the Center for Strategic and Budgetary Assessments, says bluntly. Until recently, nuclear trends looked encouraging. President [John F.] Kennedy and others in the early 1960's expected dozens of countries to develop atomic weapons quickly, but in

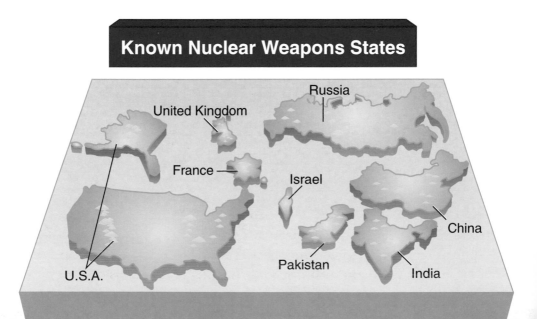

Known Nuclear Weapons States

Russia

United Kingdom

France

Israel

China

U.S.A.

Pakistan

India

Iranian workers perform maintenance at a nuclear facility near Tehran. The U.S. government regards Iran's nuclear technology as a threat to global security.

fact controls largely worked. Even now, only eight nations definitely possess nuclear weapons.

And there's more good news. While I believe that the invasion of Iraq [in 2003] was a mistake, at least Saddam Hussein won't be making warheads soon. Likewise, partly thanks to Mr. Bush's saber-rattling, Libya is abandoning its weapons program.

But all in all, the risks of a nuclear 9/11 are increasing. "I wouldn't be at all surprised if nuclear weapons are used over the next 15 or 20 years," said Bruce Blair, president of the Center for Defense Information, "first and foremost by a terrorist group that gets its hands on a Russian nuclear weapon or a Pakistani nuclear weapon."

Rogue Nations Spread Weapons

One of our biggest setbacks is in North Korea. Thanks to the ineptitude of hard-liners in Mr. Bush's administration, and their refusal to engage in meaningful negotiations, North Korea is going all-out to

U.S. and Russian officers inspect a unit used to transport nuclear materials. Some people argue that securing nuclear facilities in Russia is of paramount importance.

make warheads. It may have just made six new nuclear weapons. Then there's Iran, which has sought nuclear weapons since the days of the shah [in the 1970s] and whose nuclear program seems to have public support. "I'm not sure there is a way to get an Iranian government to give it up," a senior American official said.

Finally, there's the real rogue nation of proliferation, Pakistan. We know that Abdul Qadeer Khan, the Islamist father of Pakistan's bomb, peddled materials to Libya and North Korea, and we don't know who else.

"It may be that A.Q. Khan & Associates already have passed bomb-grade nuclear fuel to the Qaeda, and we are in for the worst," warns Paul Leventhal, founding president of the Nuclear Control Institute. It's mystifying that the administration hasn't leaned on Pakistan to make Dr. Khan available for interrogation to ensure that his network is entirely closed. Several experts on Pakistan told me they believe that the administration has been so restrained because its top priority isn't combating nuclear proliferation—it's getting President Pervez Musharraf's help in arresting Osama bin Laden before the November [2004 presidential] election.

Another puzzle is why an administration that spends hundreds of billions of dollars in Iraq doesn't try harder to secure uranium and plutonium in Russia and elsewhere. The bipartisan program to secure weapons of mass destruction is starved for funds—but Mr. Bush is proposing a $41 million cut in "cooperative threat reduction" with Russia.

Avoid a Nuclear Wake-Up Call

"We're at this crucial point," warns Joseph Cirincione of the Carnegie Endowment for International Peace. "And how we handle these situations in the next couple of years will tell us whether the nuclear threat shrinks or explodes. Perhaps literally."

The steps that are needed, like negotiating seriously with North Korea and securing sites in Russia, aren't as dramatic as bombing Baghdad [Iraq]. But unless we act more aggressively, we will get a wake-up call from a nuclear explosion or, more likely, a "dirty bomb" that uses radioactive materials routinely lying around hospitals and factories. To clarify the stakes, here's a scenario from the Federation of American Scientists for a modest terrorist incident:

A stick of cobalt, an inch thick and a foot long, is taken from among hundreds of such sticks at a food irradiation plant. It is blown up with just 10 pounds of explosives in a "dirty bomb" at the lower tip of Manhattan, with a one-mile-per-hour breeze blowing. Some 1,000 square kilometers in three states is contaminated, and some areas of New York City become uninhabitable for decades.

EVALUATING THE AUTHOR'S TECHNIQUE:

In the viewpoint you just read, the author creates a doomsday scenario to underscore the potential devastation of a nuclear attack. How do you think this technique helps the author make his argument? Do you think it is legitimate for authors to use hypothetical situations to make their cases? Why or why not?

CHAPTER 2

What Causes Terrorism?

A hooded Palestinian militant stands guard in the street near a refugee camp in the Gaza Strip.

Despair and Poverty Cause Terrorism

Tammuz Tabriz

"Suicide bombers . . . are victims of an unending psychological trauma, suffering exile in their own homeland."

In the following viewpoint, Tammuz Tabriz argues that terrorists are motivated by extreme despair and poverty. He describes the miserable conditions of life in the West Bank and Gaza Strip, the Palestinian territories where many suicide bombers originate. In these places, he argues, Palestinians live under a brutal occupation that is defined by endless death, isolation, and oppression. He asserts that these realities create an unbearable existence for people, and they thus turn to terrorism to express their rage and misery. The author concludes by stating that it is critical for outsiders to understand the mind-set of terrorists in order to end terrorism.

Tammuz Tabriz is on the executive committee at Arab Media Watch, a British-based organization that provides news reports and editorials on various Arab issues.

AS YOU READ, CONSIDER THE FOLLOWING QUESTIONS:

1. According to the author, why do Palestinians suffer from an identity crisis?
2. Why was Dr. Jenny Tonge criticized for her statement about suicide bombers, according to Tabriz?
3. According to the author, what do many suicide bombers have in common?

S uicide bombing is terrorism. Terrorism is wrong. End of discussion. This is how some commentators and politicians would like to deal with the thorny issue of people who prefer gruesome self-combustion to a life of misery and despair.

On one level, they are correct: blowing other people up is clearly immoral, and, however bad things are, two wrongs don't make a right. Violent retribution can never be a political solution and must be rejected. But on another level, the situation is hardly black and white; it is, in fact, a very murky shade of grey. This is the valuable point that [British politician] Dr. Jenny Tonge tried to emphasize at a recent Palestine Solidarity Campaign lobby of Parliament, unaware that her comments would be so badly misconstrued and that her party would so conspicuously fail to support her.

Her exact words were: "This particular brand of terrorism, the suicide bomber, is truly born out of desperation. Many, many people criticize; many, many people say it is just another form of terrorism, but I can understand and I am a fairly emotional person, and I am a mother and a grandmother. I think if I had to live in that situation, and I say this advisedly, I might just consider becoming one myself. And that is a terrible thing to say."

No doubt it is, indeed, a terrible thing to say. But it is also stating the obvious about a terrible conflict which has pushed people to extremes. Clearly, she is not advocating terrorism. The perception of her as a terrorist sympathiser owes more to the knee-jerk reaction in the media and in her own party than to what she actually said, which was not sympathy but understanding. Amidst the furor, she clarified this by saying: "I'm trying very hard to understand what makes them do that and what desperation makes them behave in that way."

Far from overstepping the mark, Ms. Tonge raised a long overdue debate. You cannot issue blanket condemnations of suicide bombing without a comprehensive awareness of the context in which it occurs. Contrary to what some observers may sweepingly assert about some

FAST FACT

According to a 2004 survey by the United Nations, 3 out of every 4 Palestinians live in poverty, subsisting on less than $2.10 per day.

A young Palestinian man is stopped by authorities before he is able to detonate the pack of explosives he has strapped to his midsection.

inherent flaw deep in the Palestinian national character, this phenomenon arises not out of a political vacuum but out of very specific, historical circumstances.

The Palestinian Identity Crisis

These circumstances, which have largely been ignored by Tonge's critics, are the illegal military occupation of Palestinian territory and the enduring human rights abuses of the occupying power [that is,

Israel]. This is no ordinary situation: it is a brutal 37-year asphyxiation of Palestinian society.[1] The ulterior aim—couched in the slippery language of 'security'—is manifestly to crush the Palestinians into surrender.

Those who reject serious discussion of the suicide bombing phenomenon often fail to comprehend the nature of the conflict itself. . . . Palestinians living under occupation experience a shattering alienation from their selves, constantly struggling to reconcile their deep sense of belonging to the land with their brutal severance from it. In short, the land is an inextricable part of their selves. It follows logically that separating them from their land will have catastrophic repercussions. This is why the most famous Palestinian poet, Mahmoud Darwish, has spoken of the loss of his land as no different from the loss of limbs. In the same way, the annihilation of the suicide bomber's self is the prelude to the bloody annihilation of his body.

Palestinians are living in exile wherever they are, whether in the Holy Land or in the diaspora [outside Palestine], divorced from their own true identity. This creates a very volatile existential problem. . . . Suicide bombing has been interpreted as a desperate attempt to restore this identity [that has been lost because Palestinians have been separated from their land]. In this context, it is worth remembering the words of the great Jewish thinker Walter Benjamin: "Humanity's alienation from itself has reached a point which drives it to look upon its own self-destruction as an act of aesthetic beauty in itself, and one of the first order.". . .

An Unending Psychological Trauma

The despair of lacking coherent selfhood is terrible enough, but more often than not, this is compounded by the murder of close relatives and friends. A large proportion of suicide bombers have had a member of their immediate family killed by Israeli forces. This is the reason most often adduced for the attacks, but in fact it is merely the spark that lights the fuse. The destruction of identity is the underlying cause.

1. The author is referring to the controversial Israeli-Palestinian conflict, which began when Israel was founded in 1948, and escalated in 1967 when Israel acquired the Palestinian territories known as the West Bank and Gaza Strip. Since then, Palestinians have lived in abject poverty and cyclical violence under the Israeli military; meanwhile, Israeli citizens have been terrorized by Palestinian suicide bombers who frequently cross into Israel and blow themselves up in protest of the occupation.

When your self has been destroyed psychologically, it is not so great a step to destroy it physically. It comes down to a choice between what is perceived as a meaningless life and a meaningful death. It is true that we have reached a dark day when we see people taking a perverse pride in obliterating their own lives and those of others, but this is all the more reason why the root problem must be both acknowledged and addressed. That senior politicians have trouble enough with even the first of these is cause for considerable concern. Is not the first step in eliminating something to accept the fact that it exists? Understanding the problem is an integral part of finding a solution, and this is true of the occupation just as it is of suicide bombing. . . .

Suicide bombers—whatever the deplorable cruelty of their actions— are victims of an unending psychological trauma suffering exile in their own homeland. Brutality, humiliation, confinement and death are part of everyday life. Add to that the well-known provocation of

A Palestinian girl wears a suicide bomber's belt rigged with dummy explosives during a 2002 Hamas rally in Lebanon.

Police armed with machine guns maintain order as a group of Palestinians marches during a funeral procession for a man killed by Israeli forces.

the occupying forces and is it any surprise the result is explosive? Palestinians are human beings; all human beings have limits. In such a situation, they are confronted starkly with [French writer and philosopher Albert] Camus' existential dilemma: "There is but one truly serious philosophical problem, and that is suicide. Judging whether life is or is not worth living amounts to answering the fundamental question of philosophy."

This is how it can appear in such extreme conditions: the daily burden of life entails loss, exile, fear, confusion, sterility, vulnerability, meaninglessness, despair. Death, however, begins to take on a different significance than that to which we are accustomed. It can come to signify safety, release, freedom, purity, meaning and, at a religious level, even salvation and union with God. This is where wider, cultural issues like Islamic extremism can add fuel to an already raging political fire, raising the narrative to a new level.

EVALUATING THE AUTHOR'S APPROACH:

In the viewpoint you just read, the author attempts to understand the people who live under difficult conditions in the Palestinian territories. As he mentions, however, many people oppose expressing any sympathy for terrorists, no matter what their situation is. Why do you think the author feels it is important to understand the plight of the Palestinians? After reading this article, do you believe terrorism is ever justified? Why or why not?

Despair and Poverty Do Not Cause Terrorism

Robert J. Barro

"The September 11 hijackers came mostly from Saudi Arabia, a country that has reasonably high levels of per capita income and schooling."

In the following viewpoint, Robert J. Barro argues that contrary to popular opinion poverty and despair do not breed terrorism, and thus attempts to eradicate poverty in the world will not reduce terrorism. Instead, he argues that many terrorists have emerged from prosperous countries and have received above-average educations. For example, according to the author, terrorists of the Lebanon-based terrorist group Hezbollah tend to be more educated and affluent than their fellow Lebanese citizens. Furthermore, the author continues, supporters of terrorism also tend to be employed and educated members of society. The author argues that these trends debunk the idea that terrorism is the result of poverty and despair, and thus he recommends that the United States find alternative solutions to terrorism that take this important information into account.

Robert J. Barro is a professor of economics at Harvard University. In addition to authoring more than ten books as well as numerous articles, he frequently writes columns for *Business Week,* from which the following viewpoint is taken.

AS YOU READ, CONSIDER THE FOLLOWING QUESTIONS:
1. According to the author, what is the general economic situation in Saudi Arabia?
2. Where did the June 2001 terrorist attack that killed twenty-one people take place, according to Barro?
3. What three terrorist groups does the author mention that were considered in the 1983 study by Charles Russell and Bowman Miller?

S o far, the U.S. war on terrorism has focused on military action against identified terrorists and on improvements in domestic and international security. However, many argue that longer-term improvements depend on lessening the root causes of terrorism, especially poverty and low education. For example, writing in *Business Week* in December [2001], [Professor] Laura D'Andrea Tyson argued: "We live in a world of unprecedented opulence and remarkable deprivation, a world so interconnected that poverty and

A young Pakistani boy reads from the Koran at a madrassa. Madrassas are Islamic schools, usually affiliated with a mosque, where Muslims obtain a religious education.

despair in a remote region can harbor a network of terrorism dedicated to our destruction. In such a world, our prosperity and freedom at home increasingly depend on the successful development of countries like Afghanistan." According to this view, a lasting reduction in terrorism entails increases in the levels of income and education in poor countries.

Many Terrorists Are Educated and Well Off

But is this view correct? One hint it may be wrong is that the September 11 hijackers came mostly from Saudi Arabia, a country that has reasonably high levels of per capita income and schooling. Therefore, terrorists need not come from the most economically deprived segments of society. A study at Princeton University by Alan Krueger and Jitka Maleckova, called "Education, Poverty, Political Violence and Terrorism: Is There a Causal Connection?" argues this point. . . . One piece of the Krueger-Maleckova evidence involves 129 members of Hezbollah who died in action, mostly against Israel,

from 1982 to 1994. Hezbollah is now designated by the U.S. as a terrorist organization. Biographical information from the Hezbollah newspaper *al-Ahd* indicates that the fighters who died were, on average, more educated and less impoverished than the Lebanese population of comparable age and regional origin.

A similar finding applies on the other side of the Israeli-Palestinian conflict to Israeli Jewish extremists who attacked Palestinians in the West Bank in the late '70s and early '80s. Many of the extremists were Gush Emunim members. A list of 27 of the Israeli terrorists reveals a pattern of high education and high-paying occupations.

Supporters of Terrorism Are Also Well Off

Krueger and Maleckova also examine surveys conducted in December [2001] with Palestinians in the [Palestinian territories] West Bank and Gaza. These polls tell us about who supports terrorism, as opposed to

Armed with a machine gun, the first female suicide bomber from Hamas (she blew herself up in 2004) poses for a photo with her daughter, who is holding a small rocket.

who are the terrorists. One set of answers reveals a high level of support for the general policy of attacking Israeli targets. This support is stronger among the literate than the illiterate. In another question, a remarkable 80% of respondents thought that the suicide bombing in June [2001] that killed 21 youths in a Tel Aviv [Israel] nightclub was not terrorism.

Some Palestinians believe suicide bombing is an appropriate response to Israeli attacks on Palestinian refugee camps like the Khan Younis camp, destroyed by the Israeli military in August 2004.

(The respondents recognized overwhelmingly that this act was regarded as terrorism by international opinion.) Moreover, the Palestinians' adherence to the view that the mass murder of civilians was not terrorism was independent of education and higher among those working than unemployed. Hence, support for terrorism was not reduced by increases in education and income.

The same patterns apply outside of the Middle East. For example, a study by Charles Russell and Bowman Miller (reprinted in the 1983 book *Perspectives on Terrorism*) considered 18 revolutionary groups, including the Japanese Red Army, Germany's Baader-Meinhof Gang, and Italy's Red Brigades. The authors found that "the vast majority of those individuals involved in terrorist activities as cadres or leaders is quite well-educated. In fact, approximately two-thirds of those identified terrorists are persons with some university training, [and] well over two-thirds of these individuals came from the middle or upper classes in their respective nations or areas."

I can only conjecture about why terrorists tend to have relatively high levels of education and income. One likely explanation is that the poorest, least-educated persons make relatively ineffective terrorists. It is also likely that some forms of education, such as those practiced in the West Bank and Gaza and other parts of the Middle East, tend to promote terrorism.[1]

The main message is that it is naive to think that increases in income and education will, by themselves, lower international terrorism. The goal of reducing poverty remains laudable, but on grounds other than fighting terrorism. To find a lasting solution for the terrorism problem, we have to continue to look elsewhere.

EVALUATING THE AUTHORS' CONCLUSIONS:

Authors Tammuz Tabriz and Robert J. Barro come to vastly different conclusions about what types of people become terrorists. Tabriz argues that poverty causes terrorism, yet Barro claims that terrorists are largely well educated and employed. Why do you think the two authors arrived at such different conclusions? After reading both viewpoints, do you believe that economics is a factor in a person's decision to commit terrorism? Explain your reasoning.

1. The author is referring to Islamic schools known as madrassas. Madrassas are common in certain parts of the Middle East and frequently teach radical ideologies that support terrorism.

Religious Fanaticism Causes Terrorism

Andrew C. McCarthy

In the following viewpoint, Andrew C. McCarthy argues that religious fanaticism is responsible for motivating terrorists. He cites more than five terrorist acts in recent history that have been planned and executed by militant Muslims. He argues that the United States has mistakenly declared a war on terrorism, when in fact it should have declared a war on fanatical religious movements such as militant Islam. McCarthy warns that until the United States identifies, acknowledges, and defeats militant Islam, it will continue to be the victim of terrorist attacks perpetrated by militant Muslims.

Andrew C. McCarthy is a former chief assistant U.S. attorney. In 1995, he led the prosecution of Sheik Omar Abdel Rahman and others for the 1993 attack on the New York World Trade Center.

"Militant Islam murders repeatedly, unabashedly, and globally."

AS YOU READ, CONSIDER THE FOLLOWING QUESTIONS:
1. What three attacks does the author list that were perpetrated by Islamic militants in the 1990s?
2. How many sailors were killed in the 2000 attack on the USS *Cole*, according to McCarthy?
3. According to the author, why has militant Islam not been clearly identified as the focus of the war on terror?

*A*llahu akbar! It has become a drumbeat, a soundtrack of atrocity. *Allahu akbar! God is great!* Not a celebration of divine bounty and mercy. Instead, their antithesis, the relentless coda of terror. Not just any kind of terror, but a terror sprung from a very particular and poisonous fount—militant Islam, the central challenge of our age.

A Decade of Muslim Terrorism

The wild-eyed chant—*Allahu akbar!*—should have seared into the American consciousness in 1994, when the first Islamic militants to crave destruction of New York City's Twin Towers were sentenced. At high noon on February 26, 1993, they had detonated a powerful urea nitrate bomb as well over 50,000 innocents packed the World Trade Center complex. Miraculously, only six (including a pregnant woman) were killed. The bombing, however, served as militant Islam's declaration of war against America, and the jihadists' [holy warriors'] intention had been for the towers to collapse, one into the next, killing thousands upon thousands. As a district judge meted out 240-year jail terms to the bombers, one, Palestinian-born Mohammed Salameh, rabidly pounded the table, shouting *Allahu akbar, Allahu akbar!*

> ## FAST FACT
>
> According to information from the U.S. State Department, since 1979, Islamic fundamentalist groups have been responsible for at least 30 terrorist attacks perpetrated against the United States or Americans abroad.

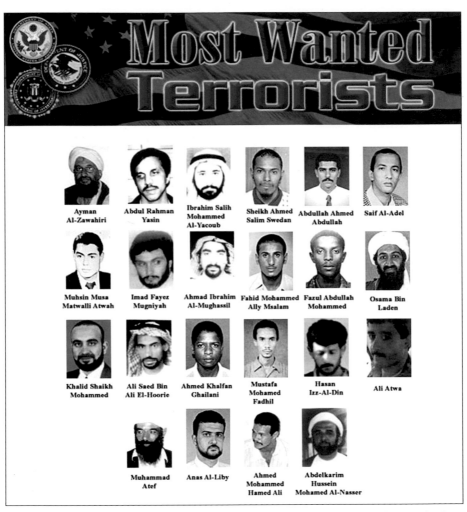

The FBI's Most Wanted Terrorist List identifies terrorists wanted for deadly attacks they committed against U.S. targets.

Militant Islam, the same centrifugal force that spurs suicide bombers to sacrifice all just to kill a relative few, had plainly galvanized Salameh, not merely in the execution of a heinous crime but in his chiding disdain for the power that presumed to impose a crushing penalty. Unbowed, he saw himself as a successful jihad warrior, his sentence a minor setback in militant Islam's inevitable march to hegemony.

It had been no different in spring 1993, for a group of mostly Sudanese jihadists huddled in a dank New York City garage, constructing the bombs they hoped would destroy the United Nations complex and the Lincoln and Holland Tunnels. *Allahu akbar,* their commander exhorted, concurrently annealing his charges and dehumanizing the count-less thousands they were bent on slaughtering—and would have, had not an informer infiltrated their circle, recording their exertions and frustrating their designs.

So it was throughout . . . the 1990s. *Allahu akbar*, the leitmotif string-ing together a 1995 plot to blow U.S. airliners out of the sky over the Pacific . . . ; the 1996 bombing of the Khobar Towers in Dhahran, Saudi Arabia, killing 19 U.S. Air Force servicemen; the 1998 obliteration of American embassies in Kenya and Tanzania, killing over 250; the failed attempt on the eve of the Millennium to destroy Los Angeles International Airport; and the 2000 suicide strike on the USS *Cole* as it docked in Aden, Yemen, killing 17 American sailors. All the handiwork of zealots, jihad warriors, some suicidal and all galvanized by militant Islam.

The apogee of this onslaught was the cataclysm that became September 11, 2001, in which over 3,000 Americans were slaughtered by 19 suicide hijackers who plunged aircraft into the Twin Towers and the Pentagon, and whose attempt to destroy yet another symbolic tar-get was foiled by heroic passengers who forced a crash landing in Pennsylvania. . . .

A gaping hole in the hull of the USS Cole *marks the spot where terrorists struck the ship in 2000, killing seventeen American soldiers.*

Source: Cardow. © 2004 by Cagle Cartoons, Inc. Reproduced by permission.

A Dangerous Denial

Yet, in less than three years since 9/11, even as the militants' atrocities have continued worldwide and even as our military fights [the war on terror] in Afghanistan and Iraq, resolve has waned and focus on the true enemy . . . has evaporated.

Why? Because, though the stormy skies now thunder *"Allahu akbar!"* into a second decade, the West, led by the United States, remains mulishly frozen in the politesse of the pre-9/11 world. We allow ourselves to see only the symptom, terror. Our willful blinders eschew even recognition, let alone treatment, of the disease. But we have met the enemy and it, surely, is militant Islam. Declining to confront that fact is not merely self-defeating. In the long haul, it may prove suicidal. . . .

Our war, we insist, is not with Islam. The official version of history is written thus: Nineteen suicide terrorists hijacked a great religion, a religion of peace; therefore, Islamic doctrine itself requires none of our attention. Nearly three years later, the aftershocks of 9/11 yet quake in the mounting body-counts of [terrorist attacks in] Dierba [Tunisia], Bali [Indonesia], Casablanca [Morocco], Istanbul [Turkey], Baghdad [Iraq], and Madrid [Spain]. Still, we avert our eyes—and our ears. With literally thousands dead and the airwaves braying promises of greater carnage to come, we remain deaf to the chant—*Allahu akbar, Allahu akbar.*

Militant Islam Murders Repeatedly

This is a phenomenon unique to Islam in the modern world. Other religions familiar to the West—branches of Christianity and Judaism in particular—regard themselves, like Islam regards itself, as a final, divinely revealed truth. Yes, they too proselytize [recruit members], and they have their occasional religiously motivated murderers. But those are aberrational and instantly condemned by the rest of the faithful. On the Planet Earth today, only Islam sports an unbridled faction that systematically inculcates hatred, systematically dehumanizes non-adherents, and systematically kills massively and indiscriminately. Moreover, that faction, militant Islam, is plainly far more robust and extensive than the scant lunatic fringe the U.S. delusionally [describes]; and its killings, far from condemnation, provoke tepid admiration if not outright adulation in a further, considerable cross-section of the Muslim world. Militant Islam murders repeatedly, unabashedly, and globally.

The war is not on "terror." The war is on militant Islam. Like the totalitarian ideologies of the 20th century that strove for cruel hegemony, militant Islam must be identified, acknowledged, and defeated utterly. Until we come to grips with, and act on, that truth, we sentence ourselves to hearing that refrain [*Allahu akbar*] over and over again.

EVALUATING THE AUTHORS' ARGUMENTS:

In the viewpoint you just read, author Andrew C. McCarthy uses historical evidence to argue that religious fanaticism causes terrorism. In the following viewpoint, however, the *Economist* uses historical evidence to argue that other factors, such as nationalism or Marxism, cause terrorism. After analyzing the evidence presented in both viewpoints, which author's argument do you find more persuasive? Why? Cite from the texts to develop your answer.

Religious Fanaticism Does Not Always Cause Terrorism

Economist

"There is [a] compelling reason to doubt that Islamic fundamentalism accounts for the rise of suicide bombing."

In the following viewpoint, the *Economist* argues that contrary to popular belief, there are many causes of terrorism aside from religious fundamentalism. Although several terrorist groups are driven by Islamic fundamentalism, the *Economist* points out that the terrorist group that commits the most suicide bombings, the Tamil Tigers, is a nonreligious terrorist group seeking to establish their own state in Sri Lanka. Several other prominent terrorist groups are motivated by either nationalism or political ideologies such as Marxism. There is no clear profile for terrorism; according to the authors, suicide bombers can be religious, nonreligious, men, women, poor, wealthy, unemployed, or well educated. The *Economist* concludes that the only universal element suicide terrorists have in common is that they know their deadly attacks leave a lasting effect on the societies they target.

The *Economist* is a weekly magazine that features anonymous articles written by groups of journalists or editors.

AS YOU READ, CONSIDER THE FOLLOWING QUESTIONS:
1. What are three groups that sponsor terrorism in the hopes of establishing their own country, according to the *Economist*?
2. What evidence does the author cite to show that suicide bombers have no clear profile?
3. According to the *Economist,* what was new about the terrorist attack that killed 241 Americans in Beirut in October 1983?

These days, there seems to be a superabundance of people willing to die in order to commit murder: in Turkey, Saudi Arabia, Chechnya and Russia, Pakistan, Israel, Iraq, Afghanistan and elsewhere. Is this phenomenon new? If so, what explains it? And what can be done about it? . . .

There is something novel about the type of terrorism in which the terrorist's death is a necessary and essential part of his act, not just an incidental cost. This type arrived in Lebanon in the early 1980s. Before then, modern groups such as the IRA [Irish Republican Army] and ETA, the Basque separatist movement, planned to escape after (or before) their

Rescue workers search for survivors and remove the bodies of victims after a 1983 suicide bombing in Beirut, Lebanon.

bombings, mortar attacks and so on. [Islamic terrorist group] Hizbullah's campaign of suicidal car and truck explosions—one of which killed 241 Americans in Beirut [Lebanon] in October 1983; 58 people died in a strike on a French barracks on the same day—changed the face of terror.

Religion Is Not a Factor in Many Terrorist Attacks

The fact that Hizbullah started the trend, and that its spread has coincided with the rise of other Islamic groups—Hamas, Palestinian Islamic Jihad (PIJ), al-Qaeda and others—has led some to surmise that Islamic fundamentalism somehow explains it. Proponents of this theory can cite the lengths to which some terrorists go to justify their attacks in Islamic terms, manipulating the precedents set by the Prophet and his companions and finessing the meanings of . . . key [Islamic] concepts. . . .

A firm belief in paradise is clearly an asset for anyone strapping on a bomb. But . . . there is another compelling reason to doubt that Islamic fundamentalism accounts for the rise of suicide bombing: non-Muslims are among its most devoted practitioners.

The single most prolifically suicidal terrorist group is the LTTE, or Tamil Tigers. In the course of their attritional struggle for an independ-

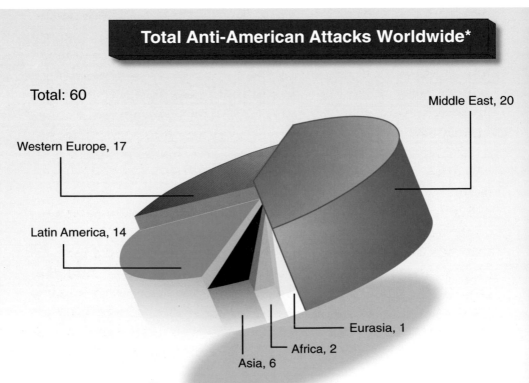

Total Anti-American Attacks Worldwide*

Total: 60

Middle East, 20

Western Europe, 17

Latin America, 14

Asia, 6

Africa, 2

Eurasia, 1

Source: U.S. Department of State. *Numbers released by the Office of the Coordinator for Counterterrorism, June 22, 2004.

ent Tamil state in northern Sri Lanka, the LTTE has, among scores of other attacks, bombed the World Trade Centre in Colombo [the capital of Sri Lanka] in 1997 and assassinated two heads of state. LTTE suicide missions, which began in 1987, are inspired more by cultish devotion to Velupillai Prabhakaran, the group's leader, than by religion. The Kurdish PKK, which has deployed suicide bombers in its quests for Kurdish autonomy and for the release of its captured leader, Abdullah Ocalan, is influenced less by Islam than by Marxist-Leninism [a political ideology]. So too is the Popular Front for the Liberation of Palestine, which [is a Marxist political group that] perpetrated the first suicide strike in Israel for more than two months on Christmas Day [2003].

Well Educated and Less Devout

Another sort of explanation for suicide terrorism focuses on its practitioners' travails and poverty in this world, rather than their imagined delights in the next. It used to be the case that a Palestinian bomber conformed to a recognisable type: he was young, male, single, religious and unemployed. He often had a personal grudge against Israel—for instance, a relative who had been arrested or injured by the Israeli army. He may have hoped to secure earthly as well as heavenly rewards for his relatives, in the form of financial donations after his death, and the new house that his parents might be given after the Israelis demolished their old one as punishment for his crime.

But the affluence of many of the September 11th hijackers cast doubt on the notion that poverty was a necessary, let alone sufficient, condition for suicidal terrorism. And since the start of the second intifada [the Palestinian uprising against the Israeli occupation] in 2000, the profile of Palestinian bombers has changed: several have been well educated and less devout than those of the mid-1990s. The LTTE, and especially the PKK and Chechen terrorists [who target Russia in the hopes of winning their independence], have preferred female bombers,

Female soldiers in the PKK army train in Lebanon near the Syrian border. The PKK and other terrorist organizations frequently use female suicide bombers.

because they attract, or used to attract, less suspicion. Some Palestinian groups (though not al-Qaeda) have also used women, conjuring up fresh religious sophistries to justify female martyrdom. Globally, says Yoram Schweitzer, an expert in suicide terrorism at the Jaffee Centre for Strategic Studies in Tel Aviv, the bomber has no clear profile.

A better way to understand the popularity of suicide attacks may be to focus on their advantages for the groups who commission them. Such operations are rarely, if ever, the work of lone lunatics. Hamas, PIJ and the other Palestinian groups who practise suicide terrorism recruit, indoctrinate and train their bombers. They write the texts for the video testaments filmed shortly before each self-immolation (making them unreliable records of the true motives of the "martyr"), which the bombers themselves watch to redouble their resolve. They take the photographs that will later appear on propaganda posters. Then they deliver their foot-soldiers to pre-identified targets. Al-Qaeda is remarkable for the expertise and independence of its agents, but they too are trained and primed for their missions.

Suicide Terrorism Is Strategic

Suicide bombing is a corporate effort: in this respect, the closest historical analogy may be the [Japanese suicide] kamikaze pilots who trained as a cadre to terrorise the American fleet in the Pacific [during World War II] in 1944–45. And suicide appeals to these groups principally because it is a good way to kill large numbers of people. Robert Pape, of the University of Chicago, calculates that between 1980 and 2001 13 people died on average in every suicide attack, whereas just one was killed in other terrorist incidents—excluding September 11th, which would make the death ratio much starker. For those whose aim is maximum destruction, not just maximum publicity, it is the natural choice. . . .

The prevalence of suicide in contemporary terrorism has helped to persuade some observers that outrages from Rabat [Morocco] to Riyadh [Saudi Arabia] to Grozny [Chechnya] are all the handiwork of al-Qaeda—just as, in the 1980s, conspiracy theorists believed that terrorism across the globe was being orchestrated by the Soviet Union. This sort of talk suits [al-Qaeda leader Osama] bin Laden; and the idea of a single, coherent enemy also has some appeal for westerners. In reality, suicide has spread not because of central co-ordination, but because it works.

EVALUATING THE AUTHOR'S MEANING:

In the viewpoint you just read, the author argues that terrorist groups increasingly use suicide terrorism "because it works." What do you think the author means by this? Do you think that terrorism is ever justified as a means to an end? Why or why not? Explain your answer.

America's Foreign Policy Causes Terrorism

Salim Muwakkil

"U.S. history helped fuel the cause of the 9/11 terrorists."

In the following viewpoint, Salim Muwakkil argues that in order for the United States to understand what caused the September 11, 2001, terrorist attacks, it must look back at its own colonial history. The author argues that throughout the twentieth century the United States supported people and policies that planted the roots of anti-Americanism. For example, he mentions that America's support of Islamic fundamentalists in the 1980s inadvertently resulted in the creation of the terrorist group al Qaeda. Similarly, the American overthrow of Iran's leader in 1953 eventually resulted in the establishment of the fervently anti-American Islamic Republic of Iran. Muwakkil also argues that American meddling in sovereign countries and support of antidemocratic, oil-rich regimes has incited anger among Middle Easterners. He concludes that American foreign policy has fomented hatred against the United States and has motivated terrorists to act against it.

Salim Muwakkil is a senior editor at *In These Times,* the journal from which this viewpoint was taken. He is also a contributing columnist for the *Chicago Tribune* and a Crime and Communities Media Fellow of the Open Society Institute.

AS YOU READ, CONSIDER THE FOLLOWING QUESTIONS:
  1. According to the author, what is the United States in denial about?
  2. What does Muwakkil suggest the U.S. military and the September 11 terrorists have in common?
  3. According to the author, what seven countries has the United States intervened in during the twentieth century?

For two days of [National Commission on Terrorist Attacks Upon the United States, better known as the 9/11 Commission] hearings in late March [2004], the public heard a parade of experts, staff aides and ex-officials talk about the failures of intelligence and policymaking that allowed the [terrorist] attacks of September 11, 2001.

The highlight of the hearing was the dramatic testimony of former counterterrorism director Richard Clarke, who charged that the Bush administration failed to prevent the attacks. Clarke's testimony and

Testifying before the 9/11 Commission, counterterrorism director Richard Clarke accuses the Bush administration of failing to prevent the 2001 terrorist attacks.

recently published book, *Against All Enemies,* make a compelling case that the Bush administration downplayed al Qaeda-related intelligence compiled during the Clinton administration to push its own policy priorities and argues that the Bushites' dismissive attitude allowed terrorists to penetrate the nation's defenses. . . .

[However,] if blame were to be justly apportioned, it would have to extend into the distant past of American foreign policy formation.

We've Killed Many More

Some Islamist radicals have declared war, or *jihad,* against the United States because past actions have convinced them that we are fighting against Islam. They have chosen asymmetrical warfare as their military method, what we call terrorism.

Faith-based suicide killing is an affront to civilization in its savage disregard for human innocence. But, in fact, it is not much different than indiscriminate death caused by impersonal Daisy Cutter bombs or Tomahawk missiles [used by the U.S. military]. We've killed many more innocent civilians in Afghanistan and Iraq in our war on terrorism than the terrorists did on 9/11.

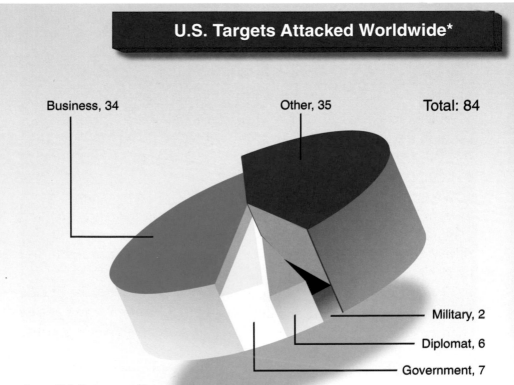

U.S. Targets Attacked Worldwide*

Business, 34 Other, 35 Total: 84

Military, 2

Diplomat, 6

Government, 7

Source: U.S. Department of State. *Numbers released by the Office of the Coordinator for Counterterrorism, June 22, 2004.

Source: Leahy. © by Cartoonists & Writers Syndicate. Reproduced by permission.

Where are the roots of their *jihad?* And does the United States bear any responsibility for nourishing those roots? To be truly effective in lessening the possibilities of future terrorism, the 9/11 Commission should seek answers to those questions as well.

American Actions Have Caused Terrorism

But to do that we would have to expand the Commission's mandate to look at how the United States advocated and funded Islamist opposition to the "godless Communists" in Soviet-occupied Afghanistan in the '80s and to the Serbs in Yugoslavia a decade later. These groups evolved into both the Taliban and al Qaeda.

We would even have to look back to 1953, when the United States overthrew Iranian leader Mohammed Mossadeg and inserted Mohammed Reza Pahlavi as Shah. The Shah's repressive regime fertilized the field for Ayatollah Ruhollah Khomeini's Islamic revolution in 1979, the first national triumph of Islamist doctrine.[1]

The West, particularly Britain, has had its colonial hands in the Middle East for centuries, and in the 20th century the United States got its chance. We've joined the fray in a bipartisan frenzy, intervening, either

1. This resulted in the creation of the Islamic Republic of Iran, which is very hostile to the United States.

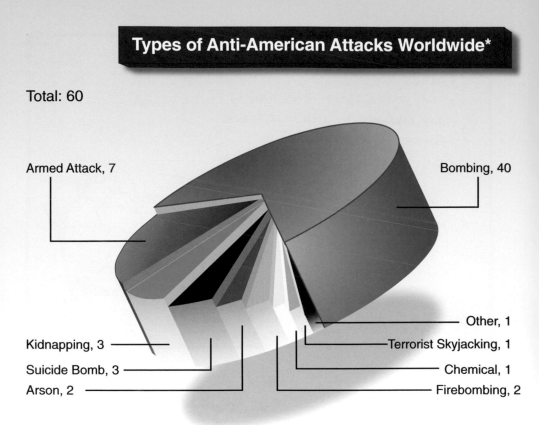

Types of Anti-American Attacks Worldwide*

Total: 60

Armed Attack, 7

Bombing, 40

Kidnapping, 3

Suicide Bomb, 3

Arson, 2

Other, 1

Terrorist Skyjacking, 1

Chemical, 1

Firebombing, 2

Source: U.S. Department of State. *Numbers released by the Office of the Coordinator for Counterterrorism, June 22, 2004.

militarily or through covert action, in Egypt, Lebanon, Iraq, Jordan, Syria, Libya and Iran—and that's just a partial list.

We've vetoed virtually every U.N. resolution condemning Israel for its barbarous treatment of indigenous Palestinians, and yet the United States subsidizes Israel in its expansionist policies and generously provides weapons systems that facilitate continued abuse of the Palestinian people.

What's more, the United States provides protection and aid for oil-rich regimes that stifle all attempts at democratic expression, even as our rhetoric drips with pieties of democracy. Much of that U.S. history helped fuel the cause of the 9/11 terrorists.

The United States Is in Denial

"Bring it on," we might say in response. If they are wishing for a martyr's death, we will fulfill it. But that's just macho talk. A hot conflict between America and radical elements of the world's 2 billion Muslims would mean an end to global stability. Peaceful coexistence is the only option.

Thus, we at least should examine the source of their grievances—many of which derive from the sordid history of colonialism. Most anti-colonial forces in the West sympathize with those grievances, and today Europe is taking steps to amend for its colonial past.

But the United States is in denial. The refusal to own up to its dreadful history makes the world less secure and is one source of the growing tension between the United States and "old Europe."

If the 9/11 Commission is seriously seeking to prevent future terrorism, it should focus on ending that deadly denial.

EVALUATING THE AUTHOR'S ARGUMENT:

In the viewpoint you just read, the author argues that American actions around the world have had a large role in causing terrorism. In your opinion, do the events the author describes justify terrorism? Is terrorism an appropriate response to anger over international events? Why or why not?

CHAPTER 3

How Should the United States Prevent Terrorism?

New security measures implemented after the September 11 attacks included regular patrols of New York Harbor and random inspections of vehicles entering military bases (inset).

Expanding Government Powers Can Prevent Terrorism

Tom Ridge

> *"The President's decision to create the Department of Homeland Security was . . . the right decision for our country and our fellow citizens."*

The following viewpoint is taken from a speech delivered by then–Department of Homeland Security secretary Tom Ridge to an audience at the American Enterprise Institute. Ridge argues that the formation of the Department of Homeland Security following September 11, 2001, allowed for significant gains to be made in the fight against terrorism. He argues that the new department's extended powers and responsibilities equip it with layers of defense; these layers, he continues, adequately meet the challenge of terrorism. Ridge says the new department has improved the security of the nation's airports, waterways, and borders; undertaken key intelligence-sharing operations; and strengthened the country's defenses against biological and chemical attack. For these reasons, the Department of Homeland Security is key to preventing terrorism on American soil.

Before being appointed secretary of the Department of Homeland Security, Tom Ridge was the governor of Pennsylvania.

Tom Ridge, remarks at the American Enterprise Institute for Public Policy Research, Washington, DC, September 2, 2003.

AS YOU READ, CONSIDER THE FOLLOWING QUESTIONS:

1. According to the author, what are three ways in which the Department of Homeland Security has improved safety in America?
2. When the author says, "The terrorist only has to be right once or twice," what do you think he means?
3. According to Ridge, how many different agencies were combined to form the Department of Homeland Security?

Today I'm here to address a subject that we would prefer had no reason for discussion. After all, we would, if we could, rewrite history and never know the pain and peril that so beset this nation two years ago [when America was attacked by terrorists on September 11, 2001]. . . .

We can never guarantee that we are free from the possibility of terrorist attack, but we can say this: We are more secure and better prepared than we were two years ago. Each and every single day we rise to a new

Former governor of Pennsylvania Tom Ridge headed up the Department of Homeland Security created in the wake of the September 11 attacks.

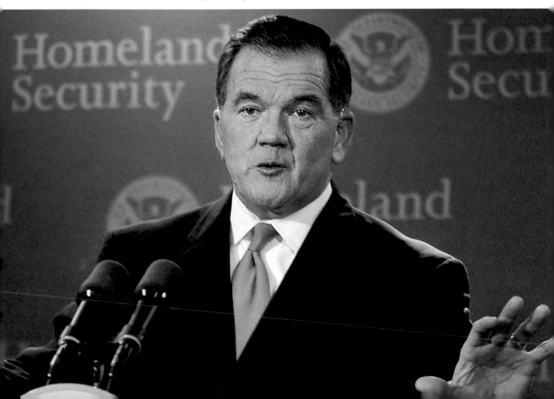

level of readiness and response, now the highest level of protection this nation has ever known.

There are many reasons for such a statement. We start with our President [George W. Bush], who has no tolerance for hatred and no patience for these cold-blooded killers, and it is under his leadership that America and its allies have exacted a war unknown to terrorists in decades before, a global war on terrorism, distinct from any battle, any conflict, any world war ever waged. . . .

That is why the President's decision to create the Department of Homeland Security was not only a bold decision, but the right decision for our country and our fellow citizens. Because while it goes without saying that we will win the war against terrorism, we will win most notably for how we fight as much as why. For this is a war in which the citizen and the scientist, the computer programmer and the cop on the beat are as crucial to victory as the general, the admiral, the sergeant, the private, or the ensign. This is a war fought with a strategy that isn't federal, but federalist, when proffered on the notion that we are all pledged to our Constitution, that we are all called to serve as long as we call ourselves free.

> # FAST FACT
>
> The creation of the Department of Homeland Security (DHS) in 2002 was the most significant change to the U.S. government in over half a century. The DHS combined branches of the Treasury, Justice, Agriculture, Energy, Commerce, Transportation, and Defense departments. Services from the Coast Guard to Customs were linked under the same umbrella, all toward the goal of protecting the country from attack.

Layers of Defense

Though we would wish otherwise, there was no single technology, no single group of people, and no single line of defense that can protect us. Homeland Security, instead, requires a combination of those factors, we like to say within the Department, layers of defense.

In the eight months since we first launched the Department, we've made significant progress towards shoring the necessary layers of homeland security that have helped to make America safer.

Information that people can act upon is an invaluable weapon in any war. Through the Terrorist Threat Integration Center, information

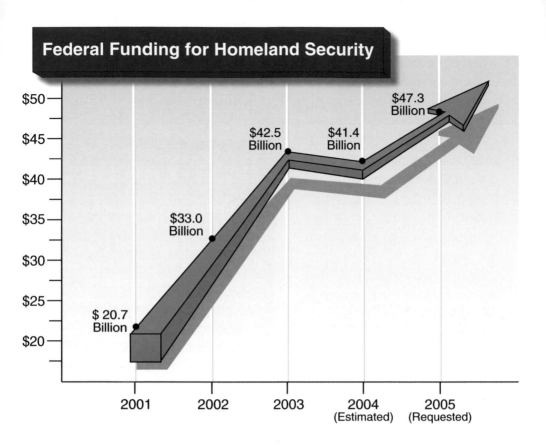

Federal Funding for Homeland Security

$50
$45
$40
$35
$30
$25
$20

$ 20.7 Billion

$33.0 Billion

$42.5 Billion

$41.4 Billion

$47.3 Billion

2001   2002   2003   2004 (Estimated)   2005 (Requested)

Source: Congressional Budget Office; Office of Management & Budget.

generated by the Department of Homeland Security and the entire intelligence community will be fused, analyzed, and then distributed for action to all of us with a stake in protecting our country.

Additionally, the new Department's Information Analysis and Infrastructure Protection Unit focuses exclusively on threats to the homeland and how we can reduce our vulnerability to attack, strengthen our critical infrastructure, both cyber and physical.

We've also instituted systems that allow us to share critical intelligence with key individuals at the state and local level. . . .

We are safer today because we've stockpiled more than a billion doses of antibiotics and vaccines, likewise vaccinated thousands of health care workers against smallpox, and installed sensors around the country that can identify certain biological and chemical agents.

This is a critical improvement that will help us save lives in the immediate aftermath of an incident. In partnering with the EPA [the

Environmental Protection Agency], the Health and Human Services and other federal agencies, I'm convinced that we will develop and deploy new and additional tools in our fight to protect America. . . .

Equally important, of course, related to it, we are safer because we have layered defenses around air travel, everywhere from the curb to the cockpit. This includes measures to arm our pilots and harden cockpit floors, the expansion of the Federal Air Marshals Service to accompany travelers on flights. Thousands of passenger and baggage screeners better trained to do their jobs and federal security officers to oversee our airports. . . .

We also continue to work diligently to address the threat of shoulder-fired missile attacks on civil aviation. This effort encompasses strategies to stop the proliferation of these weapons, work with state and local officials to improve perimeter security at our busiest airports, and develop new technologies that can counter this threat.

Progress made at our ports and waterways has also made us safer. That's why we work so very hard to extend our zone of security outward, so that our borders become our last line of defense, not our first line of defense. And that's why we build security measures that begin thousands of miles away, long before a container is first loaded on a ship. . . .

The Terrorist Only Has to Be Right Once

All of this progress speaks to why we are safer, and yet, clearly, our work is not done. The constant daily effort to protect both liberty and life must continue in both tangible and intangible ways. In Homeland Security we have to be right several thousand times a day. The terrorist only has to be right once or twice.

Every day Homeland Security works to deliver on our mission to better prevent, prepare, and respond to a terrorist attack. We pursued that mission not merely by setting up one authority for 22 different agencies, but by setting goals and meeting them, and we are, and we will. . . .

Another goal we are meeting is to increase our level of readiness and response in aviation security. Today I'm announcing a plan that will dramatically increase the number of armed federal law enforcement officers available to protect passenger aircraft during times of increased threat.

This will be achieved by realigning the Transportation Security Agency's Federal Air Marshals Service with the Immigration and Customs Enforcement. This realignment offers a sweeping gain of additional armed law enforcement officials who will be able to provide a surge capacity during increased threat periods or in the event of a terrorist attack.

Importantly, with this single move, we will be able to deploy more than 5,000 additional armed federal law enforcement agents to the skies when needed. Again, it's another way we're meeting our goal to maximize existing resources to better protect our citizens. . . .

The Department of Homeland Security Makes Us Safer

And because of these efforts, and because of this progress, and because, without hesitation, we as a people came to our country's defense and the charge of terrorism's defeat. Because of all these things, we are safer. Now, more than ever, there's a level of preparedness, and thus a level of security grounded in the purest notions of performance and outcomes, partnership and patriotism, preservation of freedom, and our accountability to its future.

Since 9/11, we have worked as only a true nation does, to do great things together. . . .

And so [with] unity, resolve, freedom and hope we will continue in the great work we've been engaged in for nearly two years. Let's forge ahead in the war on terror. That is the President's charge. It is mine. It is the charge of all Americans. It is the call to every freedom-loving nation around the world. And I join you in full confidence that we will succeed.

EVALUATING THE AUTHORS' PERSPECTIVES:

In the viewpoint you just read, Tom Ridge argues that a large bureaucracy such as the Department of Homeland Security is the best way to protect America from terrorism. In the next viewpoint, Nick Gillespie argues that large bureaucracies are unable to fight small organizations like terrorist groups and ultimately suffer under their own enormity. One author is in charge of the Department of Homeland Security; the other is editor of a journal that champions liberty and individual choice. How do you think the authors' backgrounds might have shaped their conclusions about the efficacy of bureaucracy? Please explain.

Expanding Government Powers Cannot Prevent Terrorism

Nick Gillespie

"In making the freedom-for-safety swap, we haven't just dishonored the dead of 9/11. We've helped something else die too."

In the following viewpoint, Nick Gillespie argues that expanding the government's powers is not a good way to prevent terrorism. The author contends that such extended authority limits freedom in the name of security, but in reality provides little of it. Although sweeping powers are granted to authorities to conduct searches and surveillance, he believes the public is not necessarily kept any safer. Gillespie urges Americans to view unnecessary threats to their freedom with suspicion, and warns that free societies become eroded over time; already Americans have become accustomed to an unprecedented level of increased scrutiny, and the author predicts further restrictions are on the way. Gillespie concludes by suggesting that expanded government powers do not help reduce terrorism; terrorists, he believes, have more likely been deterred by heroic actions undertaken by the American people than by expanded government powers.

Nick Gillespie is editor in chief of *Reason,* the journal from which this viewpoint was taken.

AS YOU READ, CONSIDER THE FOLLOWING QUESTIONS:
1. What does USA PATRIOT Act stand for?
2. What are three of the measures the author mentions Americans have been required to accept since September 11?
3. What do you think Gillespie means when he says that people who died on September 11 have been dishonored?

Amid the mad, horrific carnage of 9/11—amid the planes scream-ing into office buildings and cornfields; amid the last-minute phone calls by doomed innocents to loved ones; amid the vic-tims so desperate that they dove from the heights of the World Trade Center to the pavement below (what nightmare thoughts must have shot through

Protesters in Cincinnati demonstrate against the Patriot Act, one of several bills drafted after 9/11 that aimed to expand the government's powers and restrict civil liberties.

their minds in that all too brief yet interminable fall to Ground Zero?);
amid the billowing cloud of ash that smothered Manhattan and the rest
of the country like a volcanic eruption of unmitigated human suffering;
amid the heroism of plane passengers and firemen and cops and neighbors; amid the crush of steel and concrete and glass that flattened 220 stories into a pile barely 50 feet tall—amid the 3,000 deaths that day, something else died too.

By nightfall, it seemed, we had changed from a nation that placed a
uniquely high value on privacy and freedom to one that embraced security and safety as first principles. Of course we swapped freedom for
safety. Just look again at those people jumping from the twin towers to
understand why 78 percent of respondents in a [2002] Gallup/University
of Oklahoma poll favored trading civil liberties for "security" (and why
71 percent supported a national ID card too).[1] Never mind that the
trade hasn't made us safer, or that it erodes the freedom that we say is
precisely what the terrorists hate about us.

The Government's Powers Have Been Greatly Expanded
Within days of the attacks, Attorney General John Ashcroft pushed
Congress to pass expansive anti-terrorism legislation that was a lawman's
wish list (and not very different from the regular requests made by law-
men before 9/11). We *must*, implored the man who had redirected FBI
efforts away from counterterrorism and back toward battling drugs and
kiddie porn, make it easier for cops and feds and spies to get the drop on
suspects, broaden the definition of and increase the penalties for money
laundering, impose new restrictions on immigration, and on and on.

On October 26 [2001] President Bush signed the USA PATRIOT
Act, an acronym for a law so ludicrously named that it sounds like [satirist]
Thomas Pynchon parodying [dystopian author] George Orwell: the
Uniting and Strengthening America by Providing Appropriate Tools
Required to Intercept and Obstruct Terrorism Act. As the Electronic
Frontier Foundation (EFF) and other critics noted, the legislation ran
to 342 pages and made major changes to over a dozen statutes that had
limited government surveillance of citizens. We can assume that many

1. Some lawmakers have proposed issuing national ID cards that would contain valuable and private
information about the cardholder. This controversial plan has been criticized for invading Americans'
freedom without giving them any true additional security.

Source: Fairrington. © 2002 by Cagle Cartoons, Inc. Reproduced by permission.

legislators and their staffers, in the time-honored tradition, didn't read the text before casting their votes. Likewise, it will be years, not just months, before the act's full implications are clear.

Americans Should Not Swap "Safety" for Freedom

The USA PATRIOT Act is a synecdoche for the freedom-for-safety swap. Among many other things, it sanctioned roving wiretaps (which allow police to track individuals over different phones and computers) and spying on the Web browsers of people who are not even criminal suspects. It rewrote the definitions of terrorism and money laundering to include all sorts of lesser and wider-ranging offenses. More important, as EFF underscored, "In asking for these broad new powers, the government made no showing that the previous powers of law enforcement and intelligence agencies to spy on U.S. citizens were insufficient to allow them to investigate and prosecute acts of terrorism." Nothing that's emerged in the past year contradicts that early assessment.

"We're likely to experience more restrictions on personal freedom than has ever been the case in this country," pronounced Supreme Court Justice Sandra Day O'Connor [in 2001] after visiting Ground Zero. So we have, in ways large and small, profound and trivial. The worst part of the freedom-for-safety swap is that it's never a done deal; the safety providers are endless hagglers, always coming back for more. [Fall 2002's] major homeland security legislation . . . will doubtless renew the negotiations.

Freedom Is Taken Away Slowly

Who knows where it will end? Freedom and privacy rarely, if ever, disappear in one fell swoop. [Since 9/11] we've become accustomed to unnamed "detainees" being held in secret by the Department of Justice (and to the DOJ refusing to comply with state and federal court rulings to release the names of suspects); to the possibility of equally secret "military tribunals" (it's all right—they won't be used against U.S. citizens, except maybe "bad apples" like dirty bomb suspect Jose Padilla, and wasn't he a gang member anyway?); to state and federal agencies' dragging their feet on releasing documents legally available through open government laws; and to legislators such as Sen. Mike DeWine (R-Ohio) constantly pushing the limits of the USA PATRIOT Act. (DeWine wants to allow the FBI to wiretap legal immigrants on the weakest "suspicion" of criminal activity.)

We've become trained to show up hours earlier to airports and to shuffle passively through security checkpoints, to unbuckle our pants and untuck our shirts, to hold our feet up in the air while agents wave wands over our shoes, to surrender nail clippers at the gate or just travel without them, to grin and bear it while Grandma's walker gets the once-over. (Who even remembers the relative ease of air travel pre-9/11—much less before the mid-'90s, when we first started showing picture IDs as a condition of flying?) We've already started to ignore the ubiquitous surveillance cameras like the ones that watched over us as we celebrated the Fourth of July on the Mall in Washington, D.C. We've learned to mock a never-ending series of proposals such as the infamous Operation TIPS and plans for beefing up the old Neighborhood Watch program into a full-blown "national system for . . . reporting suspicious activity," both of which are moving forward in modified form despite widespread hooting.

Changes Have Not Deterred Terrorists

Has any of this made us safer? Not from our government, which has done little to earn our trust over the years, especially when it comes to law enforcement. And not from terrorists, either. If *they've* been cowed, it's because we went after [Osama] bin Laden and his minions with specific, extreme, and righteous prejudice. It's because of regular people who took the terrorists down over Pennsylvania instead of the White House, and who wrestled shoe bomber Richard Reid onto the floor at 30,000 feet. It's because, as a nation and as individuals, we showed that we would fight for a way of life that values freedom and privacy.

How wrong, then, that we've dealt away some of our freedom and privacy for a promise of safety and security. To be sure, today's America is not [writer Jeremy] Bentham's *Panopticon* or Orwell's dystopia [*1984*] (or even [Cuba under Fidel] Castro). It's not even solely a product of the September attacks, which merely hurried along trends that were already well under way. But in making the freedom-for-safety swap, we haven't just dishonored the dead of 9/11. We've helped something else die too.

EVALUATING THE AUTHOR'S ARGUMENT:

In the viewpoint you just read, author Nick Gillespie cautions Americans against giving up their freedom in exchange for the promise of security. His ideas echo those of another American, Benjamin Franklin, who once said, "He who would trade liberty for some temporary security deserves neither liberty nor security." In your opinion, is it dangerous or prudent to trade freedom for security? What effect, if any, do you think curbing certain freedoms might have on the war on terror and on American society? Explain your answer in depth.

Military Action Can Prevent Terrorism

Mark Steyn

> "If you want . . . victory in this war, there are five regimes that ought to be gone by the end of it."

In the following viewpoint, Mark Steyn states that the war on terror can only be won by using the military to remove governments that support terrorism. Going after individual terrorists is pointless, he argues, because they change too quickly and are too difficult to find. In order to reduce terrorism, the United States must go to its source and overthrow the governments that supply terrorists with money, weapons, and inspiration. The United States must not waste time deliberating about the legitimacy of war, as it did prior to invading Iraq. In order to curb terrorism and win the war on terror, the terror-supporting regimes must be swiftly eliminated.

Mark Steyn is a prolific author whose columns have appeared in the *Chicago Sun-Times,* the *Jerusalem Post,* the *(London) Telegraph,* the *National Review,* and the *Spectator,* from which this viewpoint is taken.

AS YOU READ, CONSIDER THE FOLLOWING QUESTIONS:

1. Why does the author believe the United States should have invaded Iraq in summer of 2002, instead of waiting until March 2003?
2. Who is the leader of North Korea?
3. According to the author, what does Sudan contribute to terrorism?

A year and a half ago [in early 2002] I was arguing that the invasion of Iraq needed to take place in the summer of 2002, before the first anniversary of [September 11, 2001]. Unfortunately, President [George W.] Bush listened to [British prime minister Tony] Blair and not to me, and Mr Blair wanted to go 'the extra mile' with the UN, the French, the Guinean foreign minister and the rest of the gang. The extra mile took an extra six or eight months, and at the end of it America went to war with exactly the

The chief of naval operations thanks recruiters for their efforts in 2004 to sign up recruits to help defend the United States from the threat of terrorism.

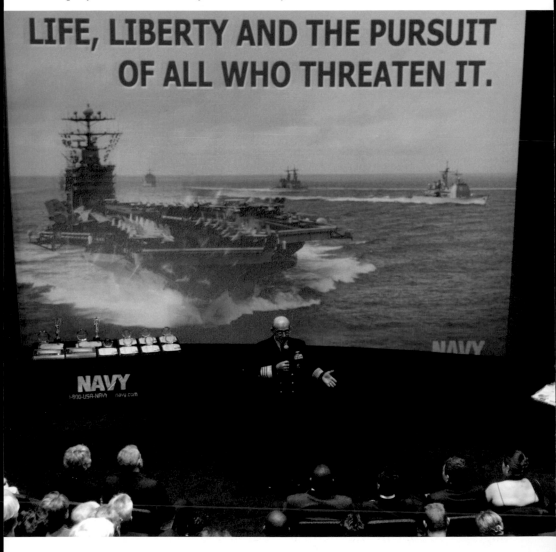

same allies as she would have done in June 2002. . . . Taking a year to amass overwhelming force on the borders of Iraq may have made the war shorter and simpler, but it also made the postwar period messier and costlier. With the world's biggest army twiddling its thumbs in Kuwait for months on end, the regime had time to move stuff around, hide it, ship it over the border to Syria, and allow interested parties to mull over tactics for a post-liberation insurgency. . . .

Going After Individual Terrorists Is Useless

There's little evidence that 'al-Qa'eda', in the sense of a functioning organisation with deployable resources, still exists. Look at the map: the al-Qa'eda-affiliated Ansar al-Islam is said to be reconstituting itself just south of the Turkey-Iraq border; would they not be just as likely a source of operatives for any action north of the border? What about the Baathist dead-enders [formerly in power in Iraq]? They're not all in Iraq: a lot of

Saddam's intelligence apparatus snuck nut [fled] in the first hours of the war with their Rolodexes intact, and they're at least as interested in targets of opportunity as the fellows stuck back in the Sunni Triangle [a region in Iraq where there are many insurgents]. Or it could be some other group. . . .

FAST FACT

Fifteen of the nineteen September 11 hijackers were from Saudi Arabia.

The point is . . . in the end they'll all have to be whacked. The reaction of Gozde Ciftlik, whose father, a security guard at the British consulate, died in the attack [on Istanbul, Turkey, in November 2003], is as good as any: 'Damn you', she shouted, 'whoever you are'. The enemy is not, as [author] Lee Kuan Yew observed [in November 2003], a traditional terror group such as the IRA [Irish Republican Army] or the [German terrorist group] Baader-Meinhof; nor is it even a Mafia-type coalition of distinct 'families'. Everywhere you look the lines are blurry. . . .

America Must Overthrow Five Regimes

So the trick for the Americans is to keep their eye on the big guys rather than on this or that itsy-bitsy plotter. If you want to be able to get to anything like a victory in this war, there are five regimes that ought to be gone by the end of it. They are:

Syrian president Bashir al-Assad is the leader of one of the regimes in the Middle East suspected of supporting terrorism.

Syria [Syrian president Bashir al-]Assad is in the unusual position, for a Middle-Eastern dictator, of being surrounded by relatively civilised states—Turkey, the new Iraq, Jordan and Israel. He has, by common consent, an all but worthless military. His Saddamite oil pipeline has been cut off. And yet he continues to get away with destabilising the region and beyond through [Lebanese terrorist group] Hezbollah: his grip on Lebanon; the men and weaponry Syrian terror groups have dispatched across the Iraqi border to aid Baathist remnants; his own stockpile of WMD [weapons of mass destruction]; and (amazingly) the Syrian spies who managed to place themselves in what ought to be the world's most secure military base at Guantanamo [Bay, Cuba, where detainees from the war on terror are held].

And yet America continues to manage its relationship with Assad in state department terms, dispatching [former secretary of state] Colin Powell to Damascus with a polite list of 'requests', which are tossed in the trash before his plane [is] out of Syrian airspace. . . .

The US should not be negotiating with Damascus; he's the guy in the box. . . . It would concentrate Assad's mind wonderfully if the Americans were to forget where exactly the line runs occasionally and answer Syria's provocations by accidentally bombing appropriate targets on [Assad's] side of the border [with Iraq].

Iran CNN had a headline [on November 25, 2003]: 'Compromise Struck On Iran's Nukes'. Not all of us are reassured to see the words 'Iran', 'nukes' and 'compromise' in the same sentence. The Europeans appear to have decided they can live with a nuclear Iran—or, at any rate, that they can't muster the will to police the ambitions of a regime just as wily as Saddam's but with four times the territory and mountains as high and as impenetrable as Afghanistan's. America needs to stand firm: a nuclear Iran will permanently alter the balance of power in the region, and not for the good. The best way to prevent it is to speed up the inevitable Iranian revolution. Iran has a young pro-American population; Washington should do what it takes to help their somewhat leisurely resistance reach tipping point. . . .

These Regimes Not Long for This World

Saudi Arabia For the duration of the war on terror, no organisation funded by the Saudis should be eligible for any formal or informal role in any Federal institutions: it's almost laughable the way everyone—from the body that approves Muslim chaplains for the US armed forces to the diplomat the Pentagon sent to investigate Saddam's nuclear contacts in Africa, to the companies supplying the post-chad computerised voting machines for [the 2004] elections—turns out to be on the Saudi shilling in one way or another.

More Wahhabism [Saudi extremism] is in the terrorists' interest. Less Wahhabism is in America's interest. With that in mind, Washington should also put the squeeze on the Saudis financially [and not purchase

North Korean leader Kim Jong Il tours a military testing range with officials. North Korea's nuclear weapons program is of grave concern to the United States.

Saudi oil]: there's no reason why my gas-guzzling SUV should fund toxic madrasahs [Islamic schools] around the globe when there's plenty of less politically destructive oil available in Alberta, Alaska, Latin America and Iraq. Watching the House of Saud tearing itself apart will not be a pretty sight. . . .

Sudan Sudan has been a critical source of Islamist manpower: its mujahedin [Islamic fighters] have been captured as far afield as Algeria, Bosnia, Chechnya, Afghanistan and Iraq. At home, two million people have been murdered in the past decade, and its Christian minority is vanishing. While this may have once been a matter of indifference to the West, it should not be now. America should be as hard on ethnic cleansing in the Muslim world as it was in the Balkans.

North Korea North Korea is one of four countries that have been assisting Iran with its nuclear programme. We can only guess its relationship to the world's less official nuclear programmes. [North Korean dictator] Kim Jong-Il has no money and his preferred export drive is for a product only the crazies want. The terror groups have plenty of money and a great interest in acquiring a product not a lot of countries are offering. Sooner or later, they'll figure it out, if they haven't already. The North Korean regime is not long for this world; the only question is whether it fails before it's in a position to do any serious damage. If that doesn't look likely, the options are not good.

The Battle Has to Be Fought

Profound changes in the above countries would not necessarily mean the end of the war on terror, but it would be pretty close. It would remove terrorism's most brazen patron (Syria), its ideological inspiration (the prototype Islamic Republic of Iran), its principal paymaster (Saudi Arabia), a critical source of manpower (Sudan) and its most potentially dangerous weapons supplier (North Korea). They're the fronts on which the battle has to be fought: it's not just terror groups, it's the state actors who provide them with infrastructure and extend their global reach. Right now, America—and Britain, Australia and Italy—are fighting defensively, reacting to this or that well-timed atrocity as it occurs. But the best way to judge whether we're winning and how serious we are about winning is how fast the above regimes are gone. Blair speed won't do.

EVALUATING THE AUTHORS' ARGUMENTS:

In the viewpoint you just read, the author argues that the best way to prevent terrorism is to overthrow governments that support it. In the next viewpoint, the author argues that the best way to prevent terrorism is to go after individuals that commit it. After reading both viewpoints, which argument do you find more persuasive? Why? Cite examples from the text.

Military Action Cannot Prevent Terrorism

William Pfaff

"Most of this military power is useless for doing what needs to be done."

In the following viewpoint, William Pfaff argues that the best way to fight terrorism is to go after individual terrorists with police investigations, rather than invading whole countries with the U.S. military. To make his argument, he compares the way in which terrorist attacks have been approached in both Europe and the United States. In Europe, detectives, police, and antiterrorist specialists undertake comprehensive investigations to find terrorists and prevent attacks before they occur, while American leaders have sent the U.S. military into countries that were thought to sponsor terrorism. The author argues that the American method has not stopped terrorism, but indeed encouraged it. The U.S. invasion of Afghanistan left that country in ruins, where terrorists can once again find fertile ground, while the U.S. invasion of Iraq has created more terrorists and fostered anti-Americanism around the world. Pfaff concludes that by using the U.S. military to fight terrorism, America has worsened the global terrorism problem to the point where it is nearly impossible to solve it by any means.

William Pfaff, "Two Approaches to Terrorism: Police Response or Military Reaction," *Liberal Opinion Week,* vol. 15, April 19, 2004. Copyright © 2004 by Tribune Media Services International. Reproduced by permission.

William Pfaff is a political columnist for the *International Herald Tribune,* the *(London) Observer,* and other newspapers. He is also the author of eight books, including *The Politics of Hysteria* and *The Wrath of Nations.*

AS YOU READ, CONSIDER THE FOLLOWING QUESTIONS:

1. According to the author, how were the terrorists who perpetrated the March 11, 2004, terrorist attacks in Madrid caught?
2. How does Pfaff characterize the U.S. invasion of Afghanistan?
3. The author compares the European and American responses to terrorism. What are three differences he finds?

PARIS—The dramatic events of [the March 2004 terrorist attacks on civilians] in Spain and [terrorist attacks on the U.S. Army in] Iraq show the difference between two approaches to terrorism. The first is the police and intelligence response. The second, the American, is the military reaction.

Through Diligent Police Work

Spain, relying on police and intelligence work, plus collaboration with police in Morocco, Germany, Britain and France, has at this writing arrested 14 people suspected of involvement in the train station bombings in Madrid [Spain] on March 11 [2004]. International arrest warrants have been issued for several others believed implicated.

In addition, four people identified by Spanish police as "the core" of the group responsible for the attacks were traced, and were surrounded in their apartment near Madrid by the police, eventually blowing themselves up rather than surrender.

This group was located when one of them used a mobile phone with a pre-paid card from the same batch as one found in a telephone linked to an unexploded bomb on the scene of the train-station bombings.

In short, these people were found through diligent police work, by a force experienced in anti-terrorist investigations because of years combating the murderous Basque separatist movement, ETA.

On April 5 [2004] French police and internal security agents detained 13 people believed connected with the same Moroccan

A masked policeman arrests a Moroccan man suspected of playing a role in the March 2004 train station bombings in Madrid, Spain.

Islamist group that has been accused of responsibility for the Spanish attack. They had been under surveillance for some time. Their group, the Moroccan Islamic Combatant Group, is believed responsible for bombings in Casablanca [Morocco] last May [2003], killing at least 33 people in addition to the 12 suicide bombers themselves.

A sweep by some 700 police officers in London and Southeast England [in April 2004] arrested eight men believed connected to terrorist groups. Elsewhere in Western Europe, police working in collaboration with Turkish police made 50 arrests in four countries.

French and British police, like the police in Spain, are experienced in terrorist surveillance and intelligence because of years dealing with terrorism, that of the IRA [Irish Republican Army] in Britain and, in France, Islamist movements of Algerian and Moroccan origin.

The IRA has carried out London bombings, including one in the City of London meant to collapse an office tower. Algerian Islamic terrorists attacking France have attempted to crash a high-jacked airliner

U.S. Marines launch missiles at enemy targets in Iraq, one of the countries in which the United States has used military action to combat terrorism.

into the Eiffel Tower (they were seized by police commandos when the plane was tricked into stopping in Marseilles to refuel), and in the 1980s they bombed Metro [subway] and rail stations in Paris as well as the Saturday-afternoon shopping crowd in a clothing store that served a lower-income clientele, much of it of North African origin.

Military Power Is Useless

The United States reacted to the [September 11, 2001, terrorist attacks on New York and Washington, D.C.] with the invasion of Afghanistan and ouster of the Taliban regime [because they shielded terrorist Osama bin Laden]. Then it invaded Iraq [in March 2003 to topple dictator Saddam Hussein, who was accused of having weapons of mass destruction]. Many influences went into these strategic choices, but one of the most important, if not the most important, was the tyranny of means.

> **FAST FACT**
>
> The March 11, 2004, train bombings in Madrid, Spain, killed 191 people and wounded more than 1,800.

Because the United States is the most heavily armed nation on earth—relatively speaking, the most heavily armed in history—its leaders automatically think first of military solutions to any problem that involves violence.

Then those leaders often find out, as they have now, that most of this military power is useless for doing what needs to be done. A year after conquering Iraq, U.S. forces still can't pacify it or provide security, and there is confidential but anxious talk in the Pentagon of a need to reactivate conscription [forced military enrollment, known as the draft] at least for specialists.

These leaders have also shown an obsession with the notion that a total solution to the problem is possible. This has simply worsened the terrorist problem, as the chaotic events of recent days in Iraq amply attest.

They invaded Afghanistan because it harbored al Qaeda terrorists. They had the illusory belief that by capturing the movement's leaders they could deal a decisive blow to terrorism. They failed to find the leaders; they left Afghanistan largely in the control of its warlords, and in deteriorating political, economic and social conditions.

Source: Gamble. © 1998 by Ed Gamble. Reproduced by permission.

With the invasion of Iraq (as the former White House terrorism adviser Richard Clarke has written), they chose "as an object lesson for potential state sponsors of terrorism not a country that had been engaged in anti-U.S. terrorism but one that had not."

They turned it into one. Iraq now is a generator of anti-U.S. terrorism, there and elsewhere. [President] George W. Bush and his advisors show no sign of knowing how to get out of the desperate situation they have created.

A Lesson Learned Too Late

Once again they acted in the vain belief that killing or capturing Saddam Hussein would produce some dramatic change. They were also motivated by the determination to invade Iraq that the Bush people were demonstrating even before 9/11, something that is far from being fully explored by press and the Congress, but which some observers in Washington think could end in the biggest U.S. presidential scandal yet.

Police and intelligence work do not provide a solution to the current wave of terrorist actions by radicalized Muslims. There is no solution, as such. The problem can for the present only be contained. It is a political phenomenon connected both to a cultural crisis within contemporary Islamic civilization and to a conflict with the United States (and Israel) which has multiple sources.

Defenders of the Bush administration—and of the conventional foreign policy wisdom—scoff at the idea that there are some things the United States can't constructively change, and some forces in current history that you have to live with. If anything positive comes out of the Iraq crisis, it will be to teach this lesson—once again.

EVALUATING THE AUTHOR'S CONCLUSIONS:

In the viewpoint you just read, author William Pfaff concludes that the U.S. military has enlarged the terrorist problem to the point where it cannot be solved, and America must now find a way to live with terrorism. Do you believe that terrorism can ever be completely eradicated? Why or why not? What methods do you think might be the best for eradicating terrorism?

Forming Global Alliances Is the Best Way to Fight Terrorism

Stanley Hoffman

"The war against terrorist networks . . . cannot be won by the United States alone."

In the following viewpoint, Stanley Hoffman argues that the war on terror cannot be won unless the United States enlists the help of as many allies as it can. He says that terrorists are hiding in countries all over the world, and the United States must therefore pool resources with other governments in order to effectively catch them. The author laments that the United States has instead acted unilaterally, that is, on its own, and says that in doing so it has angered and alienated important allies. Furthermore, Hoffman accuses the United States of violating international law by assuming it has the right to overthrow leaders of sovereign countries, and for this the rest of the world views it as reckless and imperialistic. He concludes that since the terrorist attacks of September 11, 2001, the United States has increasingly made decisions that have offended or alienated the rest of the world, and in doing so has weakened its position in both the fight against terror and the international world order.

Stanley Hoffman, "America Alone in the World," *The American Prospect,* vol. 13, September 23, 2002, pp. 20–21.

Stanley Hoffman is a professor at the John F. Kennedy School of Government at Harvard University. He is the author of two books, *America Goes Backward* and *Gulliver Unbound.*

AS YOU READ, CONSIDER THE FOLLOWING QUESTIONS:
1. What do you think the author means when he says the United States cannot substitute hard force for eyes, ears, and brains?
2. According to Hoffman, what opportunity was present after the terrorist attacks of September 11, 2001?
3. Why does the author believe it is important for the United States to take an interest in other cultures?

The horrors of September 11 [2001] confronted the United States with an extraordinary challenge and an extraordinary opportunity. The challenge was to increase our "homeland security" by measures that might have averted disaster, had they been implemented before the attacks, and that would minimize the risk of similar assaults in the future. The opportunity was to build on the sympathy and shock of other nations in order to construct a broad coalition against the sort of terrorism the United States had suffered.

Alas, it cannot be said that the year [after the attacks] was well used. . . .

America's Growing Isolation Is a Problem

One of the most distressing aspects of the year[s] since [September 11th] is America's growing isolation in the world. The war against terrorist networks that threaten the United States, its allies and even non-allies such as Russia, cannot be won by the United States alone. For one thing, we need the cooperation of other governments in arresting, trying or delivering to us suspects and possible plotters. And if military action becomes necessary, as it did in [2001 in] Afghanistan, we need the participation and endorsement of as many countries as possible. Bush Senior succeeded in obtaining that kind of cooperation in the 1991 Gulf War. A coalition is both a help and a constructive source of restraint. For a short while immediately after September 11th, the current Bush administration seemed to understand that its unilateralism was an obstacle. This did not last.

Instead, the administration of President George W. Bush has alienated allies and inflamed adversaries repeatedly [since 9/11]. The multiple, half-baked rationales for action against Iraq have confused and disturbed even old allies such as Germany and Britain. The notion that the United States retains a prerogative to act alone in its own purported interests or those of the whole "world community" is clearly incompatible with the UN charter and international law. The self-perception of a unique and benevolent American empire charged with maintaining order in the world irritates allies and adversaries alike. And the oft-expressed contempt for international institutions except those controlled by the United States—the view that only weak powers should

Some people feel that the Bush administration's strategy in the war on terrorism has alienated potential allies around the world.

be constrained by them or could benefit from them—has alienated and exasperated many of our best friends.

"We Don't Need You" Attitude Is Risky

The fact is that the United States took the lead in creating these institutions of collective security after 1945, precisely when it was the strongest superpower. That generation understood that it is the hegemonic state, paradoxically, that has the greatest interest in links of reciprocity, international law and mutual restraint.

[An unwillingness to participate in international agreements] such as the Anti-Ballistic Missile Treaty, the Kyoto Protocol and the International Criminal Court have further isolated the United States just when it needs allies most. The administration's case against the court is based on an offensive assumption that a UN institution will necessarily be unfair to the United States—and on an interpretation of the U.S. Constitution that places it above international law. Worse, we have bullied other countries to prevent them from signing or applying the protocol establishing the court.

FAST FACT

In 2003, when the United States and France argued over whether Iraq should be invaded, some American restaurants, including cafeterias on Capitol Hill, changed their menus to read "Freedom fries" instead of French fries.

This "we don't need you" posture is very risky for the United States, insulting to others and mistakenly based on the premise that others can never really proceed without us. A superpower must take special care not to provoke the united resistance of lesser powers. But the Bush administration fails to appreciate the importance of what Harvard professor Joseph Nye calls America's "soft power"—a power that emanates from the deep sympathies and vast hopes American society has inspired abroad.

America Needs Many Allies to Defeat Terrorism

The shift from beacon to bully is rife with potential disaster. Because a hegemon cannot rule by force alone, it is vital for the United States

Secretary of State Colin Powell addresses the United Nations Security Council during a U.N. briefing in 2003.

to take an interest in other societies and cultures. Since September 11th, that interest has grown only with regard to Islam and terrorism. But an American foreign policy guided exclusively by narrow self-interest is not one our allies find terribly reassuring; and it is down-right offensive to assert that the United States alone can decide what is good for others.

Particularly frightening to outside observers is the impression that U.S. foreign policy has been captured by a small group of hawks who, frustrated in 1991, are now ideologically committed to changing "evil" regimes—even in countries that have no past experience of democracy and where repressive regimes face no experienced or cohesive opposition. There were comparable fears after the election of Ronald Reagan, but divisions within his administration preserved a kind of balance. Today's pragmatists are singularly weak and seem to lack the president's ear.

Bush continually describes himself as a patient man who will consult and listen. Let us hope that he means what he says and isn't just trying to prevent a real debate until all the important decisions have been made. Because one year after [September 11], three things are clear: First, the war against terrorism cannot be the alpha and omega of a foreign policy; second, it cannot be waged by military means alone; and finally, even a state endowed with overwhelming superiority in all the ingredients of "hard" force cannot substitute that for eyes, ears and brains. Decisions based on dubious assumptions, overconfidence and intelligence reports risk ending in imprudence and fiasco.

EVALUATING THE AUTHORS' IDEAS:

In the viewpoint you just read, author Stanley Hoffman encourages the United States to work within the bounds of international law and enlist the support of other nations to fight terrorism. After reading the viewpoints in this chapter, do you think terrorism is a problem that faces the United States more or less than other nations? Does this affect how the United States should relate to the rest of the world regarding the fight against terrorism? Support your answers with examples from the text.

GLOSSARY

Al Qaeda (also spelled al-Qa'eda and al Qaida): Led by terrorist Osama bin Laden, al Qaeda has attacked the United States seven times including the bombings of two American embassies in Africa in 1998, the 2000 bombing of the USS *Cole,* and the attacks of September 11, 2001.

Ansar al-Islam: A terrorist group affiliated with al Qaeda.

Aum Shinrikyo: A Japanese religious cult that has practiced terrorism. Aum Shinrikyo is most famous for its March 20, 1995, attack, during which some of its members released deadly sarin nerve gas into the Tokyo subway system. Twelve people were killed, and more than five thousand people were hospitalized.

Baader-Meinhof Gang: A German terrorist group that was active from 1968 to 1998.

Basque Separatist Movement (ETA): This group commits acts of terrorism in the hopes of achieving an independent state in the Basque region of Spain.

Bureaucracy: A large administrative system that has many levels of operation and abides by fixed procedures.

Ground Zero: The term used to describe the devastated site where the World Trade Center once stood in New York City.

Gush Emunim: A radical Israeli group that has committed acts of terrorism against Palestinians in order to enlarge Israel's borders.

Hamas: A radical Islamic group that commits acts of terrorism against Israel in order to achieve an independent Palestinian state. Although Hamas is best known for sending suicide bombers into Israeli cities, it also operates political and charitable groups.

Hegemony: The domination of a state or group over others.

Hezbollah (also spelled Hizbullah): An Iranian-backed Lebanese group that commits acts of terrorism against Israel in retaliation for Israel's military presence in and around Lebanon.

Imperialism: The tendency of a nation to impose its control over other nations either militarily, economically, or politically.

Insurgents: Rebels, anarchists, terrorists.

Irish Republican Army (IRA): A group that commits acts of terrorism and guerrilla warfare in an effort to drive British forces from Northern Ireland and achieve a united, independent Ireland.

Kurdish Workers Party (PKK): This nonreligious group is composed of ethnic Kurds whose goal is to establish an independent Kurdish state in the Middle East. It has committed numerous terrorist acts against Turkey.

Liberation Tigers of Tamil Eelam (LTTE): Known as the Tamil Tigers, this is a nonreligious group that seeks to establish an independent homeland in the Southeast Asian nation of Sri Lanka. The LTTE holds the global record for most acts of suicide terrorism.

Osama bin Laden: The founder of the terrorist group al Qaeda.

Palestine Islamic Jihad (PIJ): A Marxist-Leninist group that commits acts of terrorism to achieve an independent Palestinian state.

Proliferation: A term that is used to connote the spread of weapons around the world.

Saddam Hussein: The former dictator of Iraq who was deposed by U.S. forces in 2003. For twenty-four years Saddam ruled Iraq with an iron fist. He is famous for implementing policies of repression and torture among his people and for seeking to possess weapons of mass destruction.

September 11, 2001: The day that nineteen al Qaeda terrorists hijacked four commercial airliners and flew them into buildings inside the United States. Two planes hit the World Trade Center in New York City; one plane hit the Pentagon in Washington, D.C.; control of a fourth plane, likely bound for the White House, was wrested away from hijackers by passengers and crashed into a field in Pennsylvania. In all, nearly three thousand Americans were killed.

Taliban: The former Islamic fundamentalist rulers of Afghanistan. When the Taliban insisted upon shielding Osama bin Laden after the September 11, 2001, attacks, they were deposed by the U.S. military.

Unilateralism: The tendency of nations to conduct their foreign affairs individualistically, without consulting other nations or international organizations before acting.

FACTS ABOUT TERRORISM

U.S. Policies Toward Terrorism

The United States defines terrorism as "premeditated, politically motivated violence perpetrated against noncombatant targets by subnational groups or clandestine agents, usually intended to influence an audience." (Title 22 of the US code, Section 2656 f (d))

According to the U.S. State Department, in order for a group to be designated as terrorist it must be a foreign organization, engage in terrorism or have the "capability or intent" to engage in terrorism, and must threaten the security of the United States or its citizens.

The U.S. government considers a terrorist act to be significant if it results in loss of life or causes serious injury and causes major property damage (more than $10,000).

The U.S. government's counterterrorism strategy is guided by four principles:
1. Make no concessions to terrorists and strike no deals.
2. Bring terrorists to justice for their crimes.
3. Isolate and apply pressure on states that sponsor terrorism to force them to change their behavior.
4. Bolster the counterterrorist capabilities of those countries that work with the United States and require assistance.

As of October 2002, the U.S. Counterterrorism Office had designated 219 organizations as terrorist groups. In 2004, 39 of these groups were declared Foreign Terrorist Organizations (FTOs). These included Abu Nidal, Abu Sayyaf, Al-Aqsa Martyrs Brigade, Ansar al-Islam, Hamas, Hizbullah, and al Qaeda.

Terrorism Worldwide

Terrorism has been practiced by citizens of a variety of countries, including Algeria, Colombia, Egypt, Germany, Greece, Ireland, Israel, Italy, Japan, Lebanon, Nigeria, Pakistan, Peru, the Philippines, Saudi Arabia, Spain, Turkey, the United States, Venezuela, and Yemen.

The most common types of terrorist attacks include bombings, kidnappings, hostage takings, assassinations, arson, fire bombings, and hijackings.

The U.S. State Department considers Cuba, Iran, Libya, North Korea, Sudan, and Syria to be government sponsors of terrorism.

According to the U.S. State Department:

In 2003 there were 208 terrorist attacks around the world. These attacks killed 625 people and wounded 3,646.

Of the 208 terrorist attacks in 2003 worldwide, there were 119 bombings, 49 armed attacks, 14 kidnappings, 11 suicide bombings, 4 fire bombings, 3 arson attacks, 3 assaults, 1 chemical attack, 1 terrorist skyjacking, and 3 other nonspecific types of attacks.

Eighty attacks took place in Asia in 2003, resulting in 222 deaths. Sixty-seven attacks took place in the Middle East, where 331 people were killed. In Europe, there were 33 attacks resulting in 61 deaths. In Africa, 8 people were killed in 6 attacks. Twenty attacks took place in Latin America, resulting in 3 deaths.

Thirty-five U.S. citizens were killed in international terrorist attacks in 2003.

Since 1993, al Qaeda is believed to have planned and executed over twenty terrorist attacks around the world.

There are eight groups dedicated to the destruction of Israel and the creation of a Palestinian state: Hamas, Hizbullah, Palestine Islamic Jihad (PIJ), Palestine Liberation Front (PLF), Popular Front for the Liberation of Palestine (PFLP), Popular Front for the Liberation of Palestine-General Command (PFLP-GC), Fatah, Democratic Front for the Liberation of Palestine (DFLP).

Weapons of Mass Destruction

The Pentagon estimates that twelve nations have nuclear weapons programs, thirteen nations have biological weapons activities, sixteen nations have chemical weapons programs, and twenty-eight nations have ballistic missile capabilities.

The Centers for Disease Control and Prevention (CDC) considers anthrax, botulinum toxin, plague, ricin, smallpox, tularemia, and viral hemorrhagic fevers to be "Category A" weapons, meaning they are most likely to be used in a bioterrorism attack.

Although biological and chemical weapons could be deadly if used in an attack, they are difficult to disperse. The effects of some biological and chemical agents can be minimized or even nullified if exposed to sunlight, air, wind, and other weather.

Anthrax is a disease common in livestock. Anthrax can infect a person by entering their skin, lungs, or by being ingested. It takes approximately one hundred thousand spores of anthrax to make a person sick.

Smallpox is a disease caused by the variola virus. It can be transmitted from person to person and has a 30 percent mortality rate. Smallpox was eradicated in 1979, and there are only two known laboratories that saved strains of it.

The War on Terror
According to the U.S. State Department:

Since September 11, 2001, 173 countries have issued orders to freeze the assets of terrorists. As a result, terror networks have lost access to nearly $200 million.

Approximately 1,500 terrorist-related accounts have been blocked around the world, including 151 accounts in the United States.

More than 3,400 al Qaeda suspects have been arrested or detained in more than one hundred countries.

Seventy-five percent of al Qaeda's top leadership has been killed or captured, most significantly 9/11 mastermind Khalid Sheikh Muhammad and key plotters Ramzi bin al-Shibh and Abu Zubaydah, as well as USS *Cole* plotter Khallad Ba'Attash.

More than eighty countries have introduced new legislation to fight terrorist financing, and ninety-four countries have established financial intelligence units to share information.

According to a CBS News poll taken in September 2004, 71 percent of Americans believe they would have to live with terrorism, while 25 percent believed terrorism could be eradicated.

Homeland Security
According to the Office of Management and Budget's 2003 Report to Congress on Combating Terrorism:

The United States border with Mexico and Canada is about 7,500 miles long. Each year more than 500 million people, 130 million motor vehicles, 2.5 million railcars, and 5.7 million cargo containers must be inspected at the border.

The United States has ninety-five thousand miles of shoreline and navigable rivers that must be patrolled.

Each year in the United States, more than 600 million airline passengers must be screened in over four hundred airports. In addition, 61 million passengers arrive on some five hundred thousand international flights each year.

In 2003, the Department of Homeland Security spent $36 million to upgrade and strengthen border infrastructure to make it more difficult to enter the United States illegally.

The United States spends more than $100 billion annually on homeland security in the form of law enforcement and emergency services.

According to a poll taken by NBC News and the *Wall Street Journal* in August 2004, 41 percent of Americans believed the United States to be safer than it was prior to the September 11, 2001, attacks. Twenty-seven percent believed the United States was less safe, while 31 percent believed there had been no change in America's security.

ORGANIZATIONS TO CONTACT

The editors have compiled the following list of organizations concerned with the issues debated in this book. The descriptions are derived from materials provided by the organizations. All have publications or information available for interested readers. The list was compiled on the date of publication of the present volume; the information provided here may change. Be aware that many organizations take several weeks or longer to respond to inquiries, so allow as much time as possible.

American Civil Liberties Union (ACLU)
125 Broad St., Eighteenth Fl., New York, NY 10004-2400
(212) 549-2500
e-mail: aclu@aclu.org
Web site: www.aclu.org

The American Civil Liberties Union is a national organization that works to defend Americans' civil rights guaranteed by the U.S. Constitution, arguing that measures to protect national security should not compromise fundamental civil liberties. It publishes and distributes policy statements, pamphlets, and press releases, such as "In Defense of Freedom in a Time of Crisis" and "National ID Cards: 5 Reasons Why They Should Be Rejected."

Anti-Defamation League (ADL)
823 United Nations Plaza, New York, NY 10017
(212) 885-7700
fax: (212) 867-0779
Web site: www.adl.org

The Anti-Defamation League is a human relations organization dedicated to combating all forms of prejudice and bigotry. The league has placed a spotlight on terrorism and on the dangers posed by extremism. Its Web site records reactions to the September 11, 2001, terrorist incidents by both extremist and mainstream organizations, provides background information on Osama bin Laden, and furnishes other materials on terrorism and the Middle East. The ADL also maintains a bimonthly online newsletter, *Frontline*.

The Brookings Institution
1775 Massachusetts Ave. NW, Washington, DC 20036
(202) 797-6000
fax: (202) 797-6004
e-mail: brookinfo@brookings.edu
Web site: www.brookings.org

The institution, founded in 1927, is a think tank that conducts research and education in foreign policy, economics, government, and the social sciences. In 2001 it began America's Response to Terrorism, a project that provides briefings and analysis to the public and that is featured on the center's Web site. Other publications include the quarterly *Brookings Review,* periodic *Policy Briefs,* and books, including *Terrorism and U.S. Foreign Policy.*

CATO Institute
1000 Massachusetts Ave. NW, Washington, DC 20001-5403
(202) 842-0200
fax: (202) 842-3490
e-mail: cato@cato.org
Web site: www.cato.org

The institute is a nonpartisan public policy research foundation dedicated to limiting the role of government and protecting individual liberties. It publishes the quarterly magazine *Regulation,* the bimonthly *Cato Policy Report,* and numerous policy papers and articles. Works on terrorism include "Does U.S. Intervention Overseas Breed Terrorism?" and "Military Tribunals No Answer."

Center for Defense Information
1779 Massachusetts Ave. NW, Suite 615, Washington, DC 20036
(202) 332-0600
fax: (202) 462-4559
e-mail: info@cdi.org
Web site: www.cdi.org

The Center for Defense Information is a nonpartisan, nonprofit organization that researches all aspects of global security. It seeks to educate the public and policy makers about issues such as weapons systems, security policy, and defense budgeting. It publishes the monthly publication *Defense Monitor,* the issue brief "National Missile Defense: What Does It All Mean?" and the studies "Homeland Security: A Competitive Strategies Approach" and "Reforging the Sword."

Center for Strategic and International Studies (CSIS)
1800 K St. NW, Suite 400, Washington, DC 20006
(202) 887-0200
fax: (202) 775-3199
Web site: www.csis.org

The center works to provide world leaders with strategic insights and policy options on current and emerging global issues. It publishes books, including *To Prevail: An American Strategy for the Campaign Against Terrorism,* the *Washington Quarterly,* a journal on political, economic, and security issues, and other publications, including reports that can be downloaded from its Web site.

Central Intelligence Agency (CIA)
Office of Public Affairs Washington, DC 20505
(703) 482-0623
fax: (703) 482-1739
Web site: www.cia.gov

President Harry S. Truman created the CIA in 1947 with the signing of the National Security Act (NSA). The NSA charged the director of central intelligence (DCI) with coordinating the nation's intelligence activities and correlating, evaluating, and disseminating intelligence that affects national security. The CIA is an independent agency, responsible to the president through the DCI and accountable to the American people through the Intelligence Oversight Committee of the U.S. Congress. Publications, including *Factbook on Intelligence,* are available on its Web site.

Chemical and Biological Arms Control Institute (CBACI)
1747 Pennsylvania Ave. NW, Seventh Fl., Washington, DC 20006
(202) 296-3550
fax: (202) 296-3574
e-mail: cbaci@cbaci.org
Web site: www.cbaci.org

CBACI is a nonprofit corporation that promotes arms control and nonproliferation, with particular focus on the elimination of chemical and biological weapons. It fosters this goal by drawing on an extensive international network to provide an innovative program of research, analysis, technical support, and education. Among the institute's publications is the bimonthly *Dispatch* and the reports "Bioterrorism in the United States: Threat, Preparedness, and Response" and "Contagion and Conflict: Health as a Global Security Challenge."

Council on American-Islamic Relations (CAIR)
453 New Jersey Ave. SE, Washington, DC 20003
(202) 488-8787
fax: (202) 488-0833
e-mail: cair@cair-net.org
Web site: www.cair-net.org

CAIR is a nonprofit membership organization that presents an Islamic perspective on public policy issues and challenges the misrepresentation of Islam and Muslims. It publishes the quarterly newsletter *Faith in Action* and other publications on Muslims in the United States. Its Web site includes statements condemning both the September 11 attacks and discrimination against Muslims.

Federal Aviation Administration (FAA)
800 Independence Ave. SW, Washington, DC 20591
(800) 322-7873
fax: (202) 267-3484
Web site: www.faa.gov

The Federal Aviation Administration is the component of the U.S. Department of Transportation whose primary responsibility is the safety of civil aviation. The FAA's major functions include regulating civil aviation to promote safety and fulfill the requirements of national defense. Among its publications are *Technology Against Terrorism, Air Piracy, Airport Security, and International Terrorism: Winning the War Against Hijackers,* and *Security Tips for Air Travelers.*

Federal Bureau of Investigation (FBI)
935 Pennsylvania Ave. NW, Rm. 7972, Washington, DC 20535
(202) 324-3000
Web site: www.fbi.gov

The FBI, the principle investigative arm of the U.S. Department of Justice, evolved from an unnamed force of special agents formed on July 26, 1909. It has the authority and responsibility to investigate specific crimes assigned to it. The FBI also is authorized to provide other law enforcement agencies with cooperative services, such as fingerprint identification, laboratory examinations, and police training. The mission of the FBI is to uphold the law through the investigation of violations of federal criminal law; to protect the United States from foreign intelligence and terrorist activities; to provide leadership and law enforcement assistance to federal, state, local, and international agencies; and to perform these responsibilities in a manner that is responsive to the needs of the public and is faithful to the Constitution of the United States. Press releases, congressional statements, and major speeches on issues concerning the FBI are available on the agency's Web site.

International Policy Institute of Counter-Terrorism (ICT)
PO Box 167, Herzlia 46150, Israel
972-9-9527277
fax: 972-9-9513073
e-mail: mail@ict.org.il
Web site: www.ict.org.il

ICT is a research institute dedicated to developing public policy solutions to international terrorism. The ICT Web site is a comprehensive resource on terrorism and counterterrorism, featuring an extensive database on terrorist attacks and organizations, including al Qaeda.

National Security Agency
9800 Savage Rd., Ft. Meade, MD 20755-6248
(301) 688-6524
Web site: www.nsa.gov

The National Security Agency coordinates, directs, and performs activities such as designing cipher systems, that protect American information systems and produce foreign intelligence information. It is the largest employer of mathematicians in the United States and also hires the nation's best codemakers and codebreakers. Speeches, briefings, and reports are available on its Web site.

United States Department of Homeland Security (DHS)
Washington, DC 20528
Web site: www.dhs.gov

The Department of Homeland Security was created in direct response to the terrorist attacks of September 11, 2001. It was the largest reshaping of the federal government since 1949. With this change, many formerly disparate offices became united in a mission to prevent terrorist attacks on American soil, reduce the country's vulnerability to terrorism, and effectively respond to attacks that did occur. The Department of Homeland Security took branches formerly of the Departments of Treasury, Justice, Agriculture, Energy, Commerce, Transportation, and Defense under its extensive wing. Services from the Coast Guard to Customs are now linked under the same umbrella, all with the singular mission of protecting the

United States from attack. Among other information, the DHS Web site offers access to the Homeland Security Advisory System, a color-coded chart that indicates the current terrorist threat level.

United States Department of Justice (USDOJ)
950 Pennsylvania Ave. NW, Washington, DC 20530-0001
(202) 514-2000
e-mail: askdoj@usdoj.gov
Web site: www.usdoj.gov

The U.S. Department of Justice is responsible for enforcing federal laws and assisting local and international law enforcement efforts as needed. The official USDOJ Web site features numerous special reports, a "kids' page," and a frequently updated news site.

United States Department of State, Counterterrorism Office
Office of Public Affairs, Rm. 2507, 2201 C St. NW
Washington, DC 20520
(202) 647-4000
e-mail: secretary@state.gov
Web site: www.state.gov/s/ct

The counterterrorism office works to develop and implement American counterterrorism strategy and to improve cooperation with foreign governments. Articles and speeches by government officials are available on its Web site.

Washington Institute for Near East Policy
1828 L St. NW, Washington, DC 20036
(202) 452-0650
fax: (202) 223-5364
e-mail: info@washingtoninstitute.org
Web site: www.washingtoninstitute.org

The institute is an independent nonprofit research organization that provides information and analysis on the Middle East and on U.S. policy in the region. It publishes numerous books, periodic monographs, and reports on regional politics, security, and economics, including *Hezbollah's Vision of the West, Hamas: The Fundamentalist Challenge to the PLO, Democracy and Arab Political Culture, Iran's Challenge to the West, Radical Middle East States and U.S. Policy,* and *Democracy in the Middle East: Defining the Challenge.*

FOR FURTHER READING

Books

Yonah Alexander, *Combating Terrorism: Strategies of Ten Countries.* Ann Arbor: University of Michigan Press, 2002. Original essays evaluate and critique the counterterrorism policies of the United States, Argentina, Peru, Colombia, the United Kingdom, Spain, Israel, Turkey, India, and Japan.

Graham Allison, *Nuclear Terrorism: The Ultimate Preventable Catastrophe.* New York: Henry Holt, 2004. A leading expert on nuclear weapons and national security discusses how the United States can prevent an impending nuclear attack.

Daniel Benjamin and Steven Simon, *The Age of Sacred Terror.* New York: Random House, 2002. Examines the rise of al Qaeda and its growing popularity in the Islamic world.

Peter I. Bergen, *Holy War, Inc.: Inside the Secret World of Osama bin Laden.* New York: Free Press, 2002. A CNN journalist examines the world of the infamous al Qaeda leader.

Wesley K. Clark, *Winning Modern Wars: Iraq, Terrorism, and the American Empire.* New York: PublicAffairs, 2003. A concise analysis of the 2003 military invasion and subsequent occupation of Iraq.

Richard A. Clarke, *Against All Enemies: Inside America's War on Terror.* New York: Free Press, 2004. This scathing critique of the government's handling of the war on terror is written by the former counterterrorism czar of the Clinton and Bush administrations.

Joyce M. Davis, *Martyrs: Innocence, Vengeance and Despair in the Middle East.* New York: Palgrave Macmillan, 2003. The author explores what motivates terrorists to act by conducting interviews with terrorist trainers, the families of suicide bombers, and Muslim scholars.

James X. Dempsey and David Cole, *Terrorism and the Constitution: Sacrificing Civil Liberties in the Name of National Security.* Washington, DC: First Amendment Foundation, 2002. A balanced examination of the problems the war on terrorism creates for civil liberties.

Steven Emerson, *American Jihad: The Terrorists Living Among Us.* New York: Free Press, 2002. Argues that terrorists from Hamas, Islamic Jihad, and al Qaeda are living and plotting attacks from inside the United States.

John L. Esposito, *Unholy War: Terror in the Name of Islam.* New York: Oxford University Press, 2002. This accomplished scholar attempts to correct popular misconceptions about Islam and its relationship to terrorism.

Thomas Friedman, *Longitudes and Attitudes: Exploring the World After September 11.* New York: Farrar, Straus & Giroux, 2002. This is a collection of insightful articles that explore U.S. foreign policy, its relationship with the Middle East, and responses to terrorism.

Judith Palmer Harik, *Hezbollah: The Changing Face of Terrorism.* New York: I.B.Tauris, 2004. This book presents a balanced discussion of whether the Lebanese group Hezbollah should be considered a terrorist group or a resistance movement.

Michael Ignatieff, *The Lesser Evil: Political Ethics in an Age of Terror.* Princeton, NJ: Princeton University Press, 2004. A leading human rights advocate examines why security and liberty must be balanced in the war on terror.

Samuel M. Katz, *Relentless Pursuit: The DSS and the Manhunt for the Al-Qaeda Terrorists.* New York: Tom Doherty, 2002. Explores the intriguing world of America's clandestine operations abroad.

Bernard Lewis, *The Crisis of Islam: Holy War and Unholy Terror.* Waterville, ME: Thorndike Press, 2003. This historian explores the sources of Islamic resentment of the West.

Mahmood Mamdani, *Good Muslim, Bad Muslim: America, the Cold War, and the Roots of Terror.* New York: Pantheon, 2004. The author argues that American hegemony has fostered terrorism and examines terrorism as a political response to the new world order.

Lawrence P. Pringle, *Chemical and Biological Warfare: The Cruelest Weapons.* Berkeley Heights, NJ: Enslow, 2000. Discusses the development and potential threat of chemical and biological weapons of mass destruction.

Marc Sageman, *Understanding Terror Networks.* Philadelphia: University of Pennsylvania Press, 2004. Explores why people join terrorist groups.

Jeffrey D. Simon, *The Terrorist Trap: America's Experience with Terrorism.* Bloomington: Indiana University Press, 2001. This foreign policy consultant details the history of terrorism against the United States.

Jessica Stern, *Terror in the Name of God: Why Religious Militants Kill.* New York: Ecco, 2003. A personal and moving account of Christian, Muslim, and Jewish terrorists.

James D. Torr, *At Issue: Is Military Action Justified Against Nations That Support Terrorism?* San Diego: Greenhaven Press, 2003. Rogue nations, the war in Iraq, and preemptive military campaigns are just some of the topics explored in this compilation of essays.

Barbara Victor, *Army of Roses: Inside the World of Palestinian Women Suicide Bombers.* Emmaus, PA: Rodale Press, 2003. This is a fascinating and easy-to-read exploration of how Palestinian women are exploited by male relatives and leaders and encouraged to blow themselves up.

Gore Vidal, *Perpetual War for Perpetual Peace: How We Got to Be So Hated.* New York: Thunder's Mouth Press, 2002. Thoroughly examines factors contributing to terrorism and the government's response to it.

Howard Zinn, *Terrorism and War.* New York: Seven Stories, 2002. Explores the history of U.S. militarism and argues that truth, civil liberties, and human rights are the casualties of war.

Periodicals

William M. Arkin, "'War' Plays into Terrorists' Hands," *Los Angeles Times,* December 29, 2002.

Scott Atran, "Genesis of Suicide Terrorism," *Science,* March 7, 2003.

Gordon Bishop, "America Owes No Apologics for Fighting Terrorists," *EtherZone.com,* May 19, 2004.

Ed Blanche, "Cult of the Kamikaze," *Middle East,* May 2003.

Randy Borum, "Understanding the Terrorist Mind-Set," *FBI Law Enforcement Bulletin,* July 2003.

Joseph Bottum, "The Library Lie," *Weekly Standard,* September 19, 2004.

David Brooks, "The Culture of Martyrdom: How Suicide Bombing Became Not Just a Means but an End," *Atlantic Monthly,* June 2002.

Pat Buchanan, "Terrorists and Freedom Fighters" *Conservative Chronicle,* March 24, 2004.

Linda Butler, "Suicide Bombers: Dignity, Despair, and the Need for Hope: An Interview with Eyad El Sarraj," *Journal of Palestine Studies,* Summer 2002.

Daniel Byman, "Scoring the War on Terrorism," *National Interest,* Summer 2003.

Lincoln Caplan, "War's Conventions," *Legal Affairs,* July/August 2004.

Marjorie Cohn, "Understanding, Responding to, and Preventing Terrorism," *Arab Studies Quarterly,* Spring/Summer 2002.

David Cole, "Outlaws on Torture," *Nation,* June 28, 2004.

Sander Diamond, "Needed: Global Coalition: The United States Can't Go It Alone Against Terrorism Threat," *Syracuse Post-Standard,* December 4, 2003.

Christopher Dickey, "Inside Suicide, Inc." *Newsweek,* April 15, 2002.

Robert Dujarric, "Islam and Its Enemies," *American Outlook,* Fall 2002.

Economist, "Two Years On: The War on Terror," September 13, 2003.

Carl N. Edwards, "The Mind of the Terrorist," *Forensic Examiner,* May/June 2003.

Thomas Fleming, "Loyal Opposition," *Chronicles,* August 2003.

William A. Galston, "The Perils of Preemptive War," *Philosophy & Public Policy Quarterly,* Fall 2002.

Helen Gibson, "New Recruits": Why Did Two Quiet, Well-Liked Young British Men Travel to Israel to Become Suicide Bombers?" *Time International,* May 12, 2003.

Scott Gottlieb, "Wake Up and Smell the Bio Threat," *American Enterprise,* January/February, 2003.

Michael Gove, "Sympathy for Suicide Bombers Is a Sign of Moral Failure," *The Times (London),* June 25, 2002.

Scott Holleran, "Why We're Losing the War on Terrorism," *Capitalism Magazine,* September 8, 2003.

Sandra Jordan, "The Women Who Would Die for Allah," *New Statesman,* January 14, 2002.

John Kelsay, "Suicide Bombers: The 'Just War' Debate, Islamic Style," *Christian Century,* August 14, 2002.

Edward M. Kennedy, "The Effect of the War in Iraq on America's Security," Remarks at George Washington University, September 27, 2004. www.commondreams.org/views04/0927=17.htm.

Khalid Khawaja, "War Will Create More Baby Osama bin Ladens," *Los Angeles Times,* March 2, 2003.

Charles Krauthammer, "The Case for Profiling," *Time,* March 18, 2002.

Alan B. Krueger and Jitka Maleckova, "Does Poverty Cause Terrorism?" *New Republic,* June 24, 2002.

Nelson Lund, "The Conservative Case Against Racial Profiling in the War on Terrorism," *Albany Law Review,* Winter 2002.

Heather Mac Donald, "Total Misrepresentation," *Weekly Standard,* January 27, 2003.

Rachelle Marshall, "A Formula for Perpetual War," *Washington Report on Middle East Affairs,* November 2004.

Marina Murphy, "Future Threats: Hype About the Threat of Bioterrorism May Not Be So Far-Fetched," *Chemistry and Industry,* February 3, 2003.

Thomas W. Murphy, "The Making of a Suicide Bomber," *USA in Review,* April 28, 2002.

Sam Nunn, "Unite Against the Gravest Threat: Nuclear Terrorism," *International Herald Tribune,* May 28, 2003.

Martha Brill Olcott and Bakhtiyar Babajanov, "The Terrorist Notebooks," *Foreign Policy,* March/April 2003.

William Pfaff, "Against the World," *American Conservative,* May 24, 2004.

Daniel Pipes, "God and Mammon: Does Poverty Cause Militant Islam?" *National Interest,* Winter 2001.

Ramesh Ponnuru, "1984 in 2003?" *National Review,* June 2, 2003.

Eric Posner and John Yoo, "The Patriot Act Under Fire," *Wall Street Journal,* December 9, 2003.

Bill Powell, "Are We Safe Yet?" *Fortune,* September 16, 2002.

Ilene R. Prusher, "As Life Looks Bleaker, Suicide Bombers Get Younger," *Christian Science Monitor,* March 5, 2004.

Chitra Ragavan and Carol Hook, "Law in a New Sort of War," *U.S. News & World Report,* April 26, 2004.

Charley Reese, "The Threat of Terrorism," *Conservative Chronicle,* January 28, 2004.

Amanda Ripley, "Why Suicide Bombing Is Now All the Rage," *Time,* April 15, 2002.

Eyad Sarraj, "Why We Blow Ourselves Up," *Time,* April 8, 2002.

Anne Marie Slaughter, "We Can Beat Terror at Its Own Game," *Los Angeles Times,* April 25, 2004.

Javier Solana, "Rules with Teeth: The Iraq Crisis Reveals the Need for a Better Approach than Either Militant Unilateralism or Feel-Good Multilateralism," *Foreign Policy,* September/October 2004.

Daya Somasundaram, "Child Soldiers," *British Medical Journal,* May 25, 2002.

George Soros, "Playing into Their Hands," *Los Angeles Times,* April 4, 2004.

Jessica Stern, "How America Created a Terrorist Haven," *New York Times,* August 20, 2003.

Mark Steyn, "We're Winning This War," *Spectator,* September 13, 2003.

David Tell, "Civil Hysteria," *Weekly Standard,* July 29, 2002.

Bruce J. Terris, "Common Sense in Profiling," *Midstream,* February/March 2002.

Victoria Toensing, "We Need These Laws" *American Legion,* April 2004.

Quintan Wiktorowicz and John Kaltner, "Killing in the Name of Islam: Al-Qaeda's Justification for September 11," *Middle East Policy,* Summer 2003.

Paul Wolfowitz, "A Strategic Approach to the Challenge of Terrorism," Remarks as prepared for delivery to RAND in Washington D.C., September 8, 2004. www.defenselink.mil/speeches/2004/sp2004 0908-depsecdef0721.html.

Fareed Zakaria, "Suicide Bombers Can Be Stopped," *Newsweek,* August 25, 2003.

Mortimer B. Zuckerman, "In for the Grim Long Haul," *U.S. News & World Report,* June 14, 2004.

Web Sites

The FBI's Web site for Kids Grades 6 Through 12 (www.fbi.gov/kids/htm). Descriptions of the FBI, investigations, games, a discussion about working dogs, and adventures.

The *New York Times* Learning Network (www.nytimes.com/learning). Designed for grades three through twelve, this site contains a number of useful and well-written articles on September 11, 2001; the CIA; the FBI; and terrorism.

The September 11 Web Archive (http://September11.archive.org). A comprehensive Web site that covers the attacks of September 11, 2001. This site was commissioned by the Library of Congress to preserve Web sites established following the events of September 11th, and includes government, military, charitable organizations, national and international news sites.

U.S. Department of State, International Information Programs (http://usinfo.state.gov/regional/nea/iraq). A government Web site providing information about current political and human rights issues involving Iraq.

INDEX

U.S. squandered good will
following, 100–102
Steyn, Mark, 85
Sudan, 90, 91
suicide bombings
as acts of desperation,
42–44
as result of psychological
trauma, 44–47
rise of, 61–62
as strategic, 66
women and, 64
surveys
on civil liberties vs. security, 81
on Palestinian support for
terrorism, 50–52
Syria, 88–89, 91

Tabriz, Tammuz, 41
Taliban, 18–19
Tamil Tigers (LTTE), 62–63
terrorism
desperation/psychological
trauma are causes of,
42–47
militant Islam is source of,
58–59, 62–63
poverty/lack of education are
not causes of, 50–53,
63–64
see also war on terrorism
Terrorism Information
Awareness, 28
terrorist attacks
annual numbers of, trends in,
33

anti-American worldwide, 62,
68
types of, 70
in Europe, 93–96
military vs. police/intelligence
response to, 93–96
after 9/11, 31–32, 58
suicidal
rise of, 61–62
as strategic, 66
threat advisory system. *See*
Homeland Security Advisory
System
Tonge, Jenny, 42
Tyson, Laura D'Andrea,
48–49

United States
homeland security funding in,
76
is losing war on nuclear
proliferation, 36–37
is safer as result of war on
terrorism, 21–22
needs allies to defeat
terrorism, 102–104
policies of, lead to terrorism,
69–71
should end support of
military dictators, 29
USA PATRIOT (Uniting and
Strengthening America by
Providing Appropriate Tools
Required to Intercept and

Obstruct Terrorism) Act
(2001), 81
Bush on, 18
USA Today (newspaper), 26
USS *Cole* bombing (2000),
57

Wahhabism, 89
war on terrorism
governments U.S. must
overthrow in, 87–91

invasions of Afghanistan/
Iraq have distracted from,
25–26
military is useless in, 96–97
con, 87–91
U.S. is safer as result of,
21–22, 78
U.S. needs allies in, 102–104
World Trade Center
1993 bombing of, 55
see also September 11 attacks